Encounter

with

Jung

ENCOUNTER WITH JUNG

EUGENE ROLFE

SIGO
PRESS

SIGO PRESS 25 New Chardon Street, #8748
Boston, Massachusetts 02114

Publisher, Editor-in-chief: Sisa Sternback
  Associate Editor: Marc Romano

Library of Congress Cataloging-in-Publication Data

Rolfe, Eugene.
  Encounter with Jung.
Bibliography: p.
  1. Psychoanalysis. 2. Jung, C. G. (Carl Gustav),
1875-1961. 3. Rolfe, Eugene. 4. Translators—
England—Biography. 5. Jung, C. G. (Carl Gustav),
1875-1961—Correspondence. 6. Rolfe, Eugene—
Correspondence. 7. Psychoanalysts—Switzerland—
Correspondence. 8. Translators—England—Correspondence.
I. Title.
BF173.R57 1989 150.19'54'0924 [B] 88-15784 ISBN 0-938434-24-8
ISBN 0-938434-27-6 (pbk.)

Cover photo: Douglas Glass
Printed in the United States.

For all those who have ever suffered
from any form of nervousness or
nervous trouble.

Strive ye therefore first to know
yourselves — for ye are the city and
the city is the kingdom.

Table of Contents

List of Illustrations

PREFACE

Eugene E. M. Rolfe, author of *The Intelligent Agnostic's Introduction to Christianity,* translator of Erich Neumann, C. A. Meier and Edgar Herzog, died unexpectedly in 1987, at the age of seventy-three, in the St. Albans, Hertfordshire house where he had lived for over three decades.

It is eminently appropriate that Rolfe lived, almost exactly to the day, just as long as his father had; for it was in fact the figure of the father—actual or substitute—that admittedly reigned as presiding deity in Rolfe's personal pantheon of inner figures.

Chief among these father-figures was the eminently paternal C.G. Jung, with whom Rolfe corresponded, off and on, from 1948 until Jung's death in 1961. Jung to a significant extent reciprocated the relationship, eventually telling Rolfe that he was one of the very few individuals who understood the whole of Jung's work, and sharing with Rolfe—one of the few individuals to whom

Jung opened himself up so completely at the end of his life — the sense of bitter disappointment and despair that marked his final months. For this reason alone — for the light it sheds on Jung's state of mind in 1959-61, when he felt himself and his life's work misunderstood by all but a small group of friends and associates — *Encounter with Jung* is an essential contribution.

As a witty, informative, and brilliantly written *document humain,* however, the book stands on its own in the great tradition of twentieth-century psychobiography. Reading Rolfe we are reminded of such famous confessions as *The Story of O.,* or Daniel Schreber's *Denkwürdigkeiten Eines Nervenkranken,* or the longer and more interesting of Havelock Ellis' case studies. In all of these pieces the author seems to be doing his or her utmost to tell the truth whatever the cost, which means in each case that the revealed history is not purely personal, but inevitably also the picture of a life in time, a mirror of its social and temporal milieux. *Encounter With Jung* falls firmly into this category, constantly weaving the reader through a cultural house of mirrors, introducing characters (*i.e.,* Rolfe's excellent portraits of the therapists who guided him through his long career of neuroticism), pulling cameos (Stanley Baldwin makes a personal appearance), and staging scenes anywhere from Bedford in 1920 to Oxford in 1933 to London during the Blitz — and, most importantly to Rolfe, at Seestrasse 228, the house of C.G. Jung, in December 1960.

As a psychological document, Rolfe's autobiography is interesting in that it prefigures much that is only now achieving (or reachieving) preeminence in the world of analytical psychology. Rolfe's discussion of "the red and the white" (*i.e.,* the Kremlin and the White House), an analysis drawn from his 1954 *Hibbert Journal* article on the cold war, neatly echoes the recent analytical formulation of political ideologies as phenomenologies of greater (inner) psychic conflict; Rolfe's musing on the psychological validity of biography presented through dreams and their amplification foreshadows the American analyst Sheila Moon's autobiographical *Dreams of a Woman* (1984); and finally, the overarching

importance of the father in Rolfe's world-view—not only personally, but in his conception of analytical psychology as a whole—
mirrors a very contemporary concern; and the list could go on.
This is not to imply that Rolfe was a visionary. Rather, he was
one quite creative individual who happened to encounter classical analytical psychology in its heyday (Rolfe attended, for instance, von Franz's 1951 lectures on the *puer aeternus*), who was
able to take a very deep draught of those waters at the source,
and whose position as an outsider allowed him to comment spontaneously and perceptively on what he saw and heard around him.

Apart from *Encounter with Jung* and his translations, Rolfe
was the author of only one book—but, as Archilochus would have
put it, one big one. *The Intelligent Agnostic's Introduction to
Christianity* examines Christianity, especially its Anglican Evangelical manifestation, in terms of the relative and symbolic nature of its liturgy, in particular the sacrament of the Eucharist;
Rolfe's contention is that Christianity need not so much mediate
the Absolute as provide a symbolic, almost metaphoric ground-
work for direct contact with the Absolute—which itself can be
broadly defined as what the psychologist would call the self and
what the theologian would call the face of God. Hence Rolfe oc-
cupies a position midway between Christian orthodoxy and its
more radical heresies, for instance that of Ulrich Zwingli, who
maintained that the doctrine of transubstantiation—the heart of
the Eucharist—should be understood symbolically as opposed to
actually and corporeally.

These ideas are not new, and in fact many can be traced back
to Jung himself, especially to his "Transformation Symbolism in
the Mass." What makes Rolfe's book work, however, is the origi-
nality of the authorial experience and spirit that informs the book
as a whole (otherwise, in terms of intellectual genesis, Rolfe provides the equation of 85% Jung, 15% other scholars and Rolfe).
The dedication for the book is a sterling example:

The author would like to pay a tribute of sincere gratitude to his

own frustrations, without whose unfailing co-operation this book
could never have been written.

Yet unfortunately enough, Rolfe's efforts never brought him the
wider attention he originally craved. Apart from Rolfe's own correspondence with Jung and others (and nineteen reviews in various newspapers and journals, whose generally positive responses
were invariably hidden away in back columns or "Advent Reading" lists), *The Intelligent Agnostic's Introduction to Christianity* attracted little outside attention; it enjoyed only a small and
fleeting *succès d'estime*. This is regrettable, for the book is solid
and erudite if eccentric and often cranky, as though its author
were G. B. Shaw and Raskolnikov somehow fused into one persona, but passionately searching for an answer to highly personal
concerns, religious and otherwise. It is in the actual formulation
of his arguments, in both *Encounter With Jung* and *The Intelligent Agnostic's Introduction to Christianity,* that Rolfe reveals
himself, genuinely and engrossingly, as a good soul with a good
mind and a tremendous amount of personal integrity — and
idiosyncrasy, as Rolfe would be the first to admit.

Sigo Press is proud to publish *Encounter With Jung,* which we
hope will at least partially draw the memory of Eugene Rolfe out
of the shadows. So it is to the memory of Rolfe (and his frustrations) that we lovingly dedicate this book, wishing him well in
the beyond, where by rights his first book should be enjoying its
umpteenth reprinting.

The Editors

Acknowledgements

I would like to thank Dr. Paula Black and Joan Reggioni, without whose help this enterprise would never have been launched. Thanks also go to Douglas Glass for permission to reprint his photographs of Jung.

The author is grateful to the following for permission to reprint previously published or unpublished works: Princeton University Press, for three letters (pp. 523-4, 174, 610-611) to the author from C.G. Jung. In *C. G. Jung: Letters,* Bolligen Series XCV, Vol. I; the estate of C.G. Jung for permission to reproduce three unpublished letters to the author. These are dated July 14, 1959, November 12, 1960, and December 7, 1960.

Part One:

Beginnings

I
Childhood _____

I was born at Bedford, in 1914, shortly after the outbreak of World War I. My father, Eugene Alfred Rolfe, was a master at Bedford Grammar School (it didn't become "The Bedford School" till 1917, when George V paid it a visit: there used to be a picture at the old home of my father being presented to the King-Emperor on that occasion). He was a fine classical scholar and a good school-master of the old-fashioned kind, though a little bit Prussian and prickly by nature. He had a special gift for teaching "heavies" (boys whose volume was considerably in excess of their brightness). His own parents had both been carried off by smallpox when he was three: his position in the public school middle-class, though secure, depended upon himself alone; he had very few social connections.

My mother, who by that intrinsic personal rating which bursts all categories of social class must surely rank as one of nature's empresses, came from quite a different anthropological habitat.

Her father was a Nonconformist of the old school, yet he'd been soldier, station-master, Shakespearean actor, and manager of a fun-fair in the Isle of Man before he finally settled down in Chelsea and invented a process for steeping wicks in such a way that the oil lamps of the period would not sputter. He was a Radical, and a little Englander, and the boys in Chelsea broke his windows at the time of the Boer War for that reason.

My mother, Rose Emily Sansom, "Daisy" at home because she was always as fresh as one, came of a family of twelve siblings, six of whom survived. She united beauty with supreme vitality; she captivated my father and married him in 1913, when he was 43 and in danger of incurable celibacy, and she a headstrong 29. I need hardly say that the transplantation of this wild rose of Chelsea to the trim parterres of middle-class Bedford before World War I did not occur without some slight difficulties of adjustment.

At an early age, I was firmly wedged in the clamps of the Oedipus situation. I was romantically in love with my mother. I remember her beautiful young face, her "nice eyes" and her very find dark soft hair. She was soft-hearted and indulgent towards me.

I clung to her for love and security, and shrank away in terror from my stern father, who appeared to me to be oppressive, angry, and forbidding. I once had a little toy suite of furniture, in a little toy box not much bigger than a match-box. My mother had allowed me to have this with me in bed, but my father had forbidden this for some reason — and, sure as fate, he came in one night and discovered it with me under the blankets. The diminutive toy box had become in some way a symbol of the conflict between them.

What my mother gave me in the name of love, my father wanted to take away in the name of discipline. The truth probably lay somewhere between them; but the net result of their disagreement was a horribly guilty small child.

The form my reaction took was determined by my own sensitive constitution. I lacked either the physical or the emotion strength to put up any kind of a struggle. It was a foregone conclusion that I would submit, not rebel.

Not that I was entirely deficient in all masculine characteristics. But these were enlisted in my mother's service, and were out of relationship with my father's side. I was my mother's little knight, and took her for rides on the arm of a chair. I used to dig enormous cavities in the garden beds for my mother's benefit, and she used to look out at them from a window upstairs, like a princess in a fairy story.

Later, I did admire my father enormously. But I was up against the tragic fact that his nose was straight, mine concave. "Will I have a straight nose like yours when I grow up, Daddy?" I asked him. To encourage me, he said that in all probability this would be so. I tried to persuade myself of the truth of this; but I was left struggling with the poignant counter-realisation. I knew deep down I would never make it. The plain fact was that I was a completely different type from my father.

Yet I must say I did not have an unhappy childhood, on the whole. I was quiet, and stayed at home a lot, and played imaginative games with my sister, weaving fantasy histories about families of toys.

I was at Bedford School from 1923 to 1933. Notoriously such schools do not provide a soil particularly congenial to the sensitive plant; and I was one of these dubious creatures. Yet I can't say that I was ever seriously bullied by the boys of Bedford School; I was a day-boy, of course—and that makes a difference.

I used to wet myself occasionally in class; I even did this once in Chapel, and once (public horror!) at gym. This no doubt was an index of my inner insecurity and unhappiness. Yet part at least of my anxiety was due to the fact that I suffered from total bewilderment and disorientation when faced with the problems of the outside world. I had been brought up to be house-trained, but not world-worthy. And behind this again was the constitutional factor: it was the typical reaction of the born introvert when exposed to the cold air of exterior reality.

I was given an excellent academic education. I naturally stayed

put on the classical side, where I was following in my father's footsteps. One crucial feature which is often forgotten in discussions
on the differences between the public schools and the national
education system is the far greater part played by religion in the
former. At Bedford, though Scripture and Greek Testament peri-
ods (non-denominational) were an amiable relaxation enlivened
by farce, the Sunday services in the school chapel (solid, middle-
of-the-road Anglican) were real and gripping and went right home.
The hymns were powerful and moving; the sermons, more powerful still, left me with a profound sense of being a sinner. The figure
of Jesus, with its enormous appeal, sank right down deep inside
me. Whatever doubts I may have gathered about Christianity (and
I lost my faith in the regulation manner round about the age of
sixteen), I did absorb certain moral standards which I accepted
quite without question. It was only much later in life that I realised how distinctively Christian many of these standards were.
Any form of ego-assertion such as boasting or aggressiveness in
society was felt to be just bad form; the impact of this flat-rate
morality was not always psychologically fortunate, since it took
no account of the fact that, at some stages and for some temper-
aments, the ego may actually need encouragement.

II
Adolescence _____

The relative peace of my later childhood and middle years at school was completely shattered by adolescence. With the onset of puberty, the physical life which had been so stunted came rushing up inside me. I began to practise physical exercises naked in my room.

One day, exasperated and excited by my failure to leap over the iron bar at the bottom of my bed, I flung myself down bodily on the bed and masturbated spontaneously. Incredible though it my seem, I had no idea what it was that I had done. But I very soon found out. This was "self-abuse" — something so dreadfully shameful and wrong that no-one could possibly continue to do it and retain his self-respect. The specifically Christian horror and disgust at any kind of unconventional sexual practice had taken vacant possession of my conscience.

Yet the thing had a fascination as powerful as life, and it threatened to get an iron grip upon me. I began a frightful lonely wrestle. I made resolution and struggled hard, but again and again (maybe after weeks) I was beaten. I know exactly what it is to be the slave of a passion stronger than the ego. I know exactly what addiction is like. The odd thing is that I was "addicted" to one of the two primary instincts of human nature. And I was addicted to it in the form of a habit which is practised by practically every member of our species at some time in his — or her — developmental career.

At one stage, I was so desperate, defeated and demoralised that I let myself go and gave up hope. A surging, passionate desire to kill myself took possession of me, and I tried to commit suicide three times — by cutting my arm ("opening the veins"), by turning on a disused gas jet in the W.C., and by drinking the contents of a poison bottle (it actually contained embrocation). I was not successful — I hadn't the guts, to tell the truth. The blood only flowed in a thin little trickle; the gas, thinner still, only made a stink; and the contents of the poison bottle only gave me a ghastly headache.

I think that aggression, denied normal outlets, turned violently inwards against myself. What released it was my black mood of fury and despair; fury that I'd totally failed to beat masturbation, and despair because I felt I could no longer hope for any kind of decent future.

Before "dying," I made a will and a statement of advice for the benefit of my family. As the death which had been arranged never actually took place, these documents were never delivered. But the advice I gave was lucid and sensible, and showed a reasonable moral concern for my relatives. My rational self, displaced but not destroyed by the demonic lust for self-destruction, continued, like a kind of partial personality, to function in the background.

As I'd had no more success in killing myself than in downing masturbation, I just had to go on living. In the end, after two years' struggle or more, I finally succeeded in breaking the habit. I was rewarded with a first-class anxiety neurosis.

My mind was now invaded and possessed by irrational doubts — that was the way it took me at first. I had to fight recurring battles to convince myself of the necessity of doing quite a routine job; with insane iteration the doubt kept repeating, "Why must I do this homework? Why must I do this homework?"

It is difficult for me now, looking back, to enter into the sheer intensity of these irrational feelings. You might compare it to a sort of *swarming.*

A phrase I used later on ("the storm and frenzy of anxiety") gives something of the feel of it. But this was already a literary formulation. I can only say that my struggle against these two demonic visitants — masturbation and its successor (and alternative), neurosis — completely destroyed the bloom of my youth.

Though technically without faith, I still accepted as part of the law of the universe the Christian-toned moral philosophy in which I had been educated. This was essentially static. Moral acts were good or bad; bad acts and habits had to be avoided or overcome by acts of will. The fatal weakness of this whole outlook lies in its unawareness of the dynamics of the psyche. The electric current of sexual energy had been switched on and was surging powerfully forwards. To switch it off by an act of will was asking for trouble. What was to happen to the powerful charge that had been let loose in my system? Naturally, it went to my head and appeared in consciousness in the shape of a frenzied swarm of irrational doubts. Might not the law of the conservation of energy apply in psychics as well as in physics? But my "philosophy" knew nothing of these things.

It was just my pestilential bad luck to live at one of those crossroads of history, the transition-period between two ages. The Manichaean moral philosophy was still most successfully propagated by the Church, a ghastly stigmata of denial. But all over Europe the religious faith — which, in its intuitive way, had contained some rudimentary psychic knowledge — was lapsing. I had the worst of both worlds: I was left holding a dead baby — the cold, naked moral illusion. There wasn't a soul among my soul's mentors — not even an emancipated uncle — who had the slightest spark of that picaresque, rueful-ironic acceptance of sex which would have been the perfect antidote to my condition. It was all deadly reverent and solemn and moralistic.

I myself was extremely keen to do something about my trouble. I was driven by desperation to get some kind of alleviation for my sufferings. I remember scraping up the vast sum of forty shillings (prewar) to buy Dr. Stanley Hall's massive work on "Adolescence" (in two volumes) which I had seen advertised somewhere. This book is comparatively stern about masturbation; but I well remember the gasping relief I felt when I read the passages about it. In contrast with the ideas I'd picked up, Dr. Hall's attitude seemed like permissive heaven.

In 1932 — after asking permission from my father — I launched into Pelmanism, which I took very seriously. The central imperative in this excellent system was that the student was required to have an aim in life; I selected as my aim a scholarship at Oxford. This concept of constructive ambition, linked as it necessarily must be with "reality," adaptation and success, proved far more effective at that stage than any help I had received from religion. It didn't cure my neurosis, but it did pull me of the ditch. I forced myself to work really hard for a term, though I still had to fight an acute battle against doubts. I won the Field Marshal Gomm scholarship in classics at Keble College, Oxford; and for the next four years (1933-1937), I lived in a new world.

Of course, I was a great disappointment to my father. Instead of an upstanding young Public School man, good at games, a brilliant scholar, quite free of morbid problems and forging confidently ahead towards the right kind of position in (say) the Home Civil Service, I was a total flop — a non-games-playing, non-starting, neurotic son. I simply failed to make the grade. He was prickly and potent; I was argumentative and resentful; and of course there was friction and irritation between us. And yet, ideologically, I followed his pattern.

In religion, my father was privately an agnostic. This meant that the positive ideas I received from his were political and cultural rather than religious. In politics, I inherited from my father an enthusiastic faith in England of a moderate, Baldwinian-conservative colour; in culture, a deep but quite unformulated feeling of belonging in the grand classical stream of European civilisation.

Relatively early on at school, I won a star for an essay on Stanley Baldwin, and later I was a burning enthusiast for the British Empire. However, this was not destined to last. It so happened that, not long before I went up to Oxford, my father and I went away on a visit to some old friends of his at Brighton. This was a new experience for me: never before, at any time, had I been parted from my mother.

My father's friends were two sisters. Both of them were old maids, both devoted, practising Christians and both firm adherents of the High Church school. One fine summer Sunday evening, one of these sisters took my father and myself to Evensong at St. Martin's. In the palmy old days of the private railway companies, the Anglo-Catholic Movement was known familiarly to some of its associates as "the London, Brighton and South Coast religion." Brighton certainly did its level best to live up to its share of the title role.

I myself was entirely innocent of these matters. It was the first time I had ever witnessed the gorgeous peacock of Catholic ritual, with its tail spread right out in fullest display. There were lights, there was incense; there was colour, deep emotion and joy. But above all, there was a procession in honour of the Blessed Virgin Mary. Slowly, this procession wound its way round the church; and slowly the choir wound its way through the verses of a long hymn to the Virgin Mary, with a slow, sweet, languorous tune. One of the verses ran as follows:

For the sick and for the aged,
For our dear ones far away,
For the hearts that mourn in secret,

All who need our prayers today,
For the faithful gone gone before us
May the holy Virgin pray!
Hail Mary! Hail Mary!
Hail Mary, full of grace!

The effect on me was instantaneous and decisive. My Protestant prejudices were swept away and evaporated in the twinkling of an eye; it wasn't until some twenty-five years later that I realised I still had some vestiges of Protestant feeling inside me.

It was a complete conversion experience and one of a very curious kind. From that moment and for the next nine years or more, Catholicism (first Anglican, the Roman, then Anglican again, but always Catholicism) was the great, consuming, romantic passion of my life. And yet throughout the whole of this long period, I never, intellectually, believed in God. I went the whole way with the Catholics in practically all their opinions and attitudes — and yet I was not a believing Christian. Somewhere inside me I was carrying around an unresolved antinomy; years later it was to crop up again for further consideration.

III
Oxford _____

I was happy at Keble in a way that was certainly not true of me at Bedford School. The School Chapel at Bedford (though I was confirmed there) is just an ordinary ecclesiastical building to me. But I can never enter Keble Chapel without feeling touched, deep down. I loved Keble and through Keble and beyond it, Oxford, and I felt deep down that I *belonged* to them both. Spiritually, I was entirely at home.

The Blessed Virgin, whose image had swept me off my feet at St. Martin's, Brighton, was really only a shining figure standing at the door. The feeling fanned right out to embrace the whole fabric of the Catholic Church. And, as always, the Church was not just a spiritual institution to me; she has to be seen as deeply rooted in the whole natural background of the earth and the land.

I loved the brilliant dark night skies of Oxford, with the spire of St. Mary's towering sheer away up into heaven like some spectacular Gothic rocket. I loved High Mass at Cowley, which I regarded as the living prototype of a pre-reformation English monastic church. I loved plainsong, vestments, old churches, and St. Frideswide's. I loved my afternoon walks into the country round Oxford—Cumnor, Hinksey, Godstow, and the distant views of the towers of the city. Love, with this rich background of colour and imagination, filled out a new dimension in me.

I had two close friends at Keble, and two or three in other colleges. But on the whole, I continued to lead a pretty solitary existence. I didn't mind so terribly much. I knew what it was to be lonely, though; and sometimes, when I was lying in bed at night, and could hear the laughter and voices of contemporaries of both sexes as they walked along in the street underneath my window, I did feel a yearning pang of exclusion from life. It was as if youth, with its gaiety and high spirits, was almost literally passing me by.

One of my Keble friends happened to incarnate this very quality. Unlike the rest, he had worked (as a railway clerk) in the world before "coming up" to Oxford. He was an honest though far from brilliant theological student. But somehow, he managed to convey the idea that gaiety, and a kind of innocent naughtiness, were built-in features of the Catholic ideal.

It's obvious that my passion for Catholicism represented a colossal and triumphant breakthrough of the feminine side of my nature—all the colour and emotion that was suppressed in my father's stoic philosophy. But this "feminine" was still very much wrapped up inside the Mother imago; the ruling divinity of my Catholicism was maternal.

Curiously enough, the one paper I read to the Essay Club at Keble was devoted to "The Defence of the Feminine." I maintained that the feminine is a legitimate mode and that the masculine mind is too hostile to feeling. I wrote this paper at a time when formulations such as Goethe's *Ewig Weibliche (The Eternal Feminine)* and Jung's *anima* (the feminine component in the psyche) were sill right out beyond my ken.

As it happens, I was capable of experiencing this "feminine" quite apart from Mother Church. During one long vacation (I was at home, away from Oxford at the time), I composed an English version of Hans Anderson's "Little Mermaid." I didn't know a word of Danish, but the English translations I possessed seemed to me so crude and inadequate that I set to work to collate and conflate them. I took endless trouble over the job; and in the end I succeeded in producing a version which has a kind of pearly elegance about it. Of course, the story is heartrendingly sentimental and *traurig* – actually an extreme case of the kind of "feminine" I had illustrated in my talk. Unconsciously, I had identified myself with the tragic Little Mermaid who was forced to bear such cruel sufferings.

In reality, Catholicism didn't lead me towards real women, even of the mother-type. The one exception was a pleasant, intermittent relationship with the mother of my "merry" friend – a big, jolly Anglo-Catholic woman, rather like a cross between G. K. Chesterton and a gypsy. The only girlfriend I had at Oxford (it was a slight, shy, adolescent affair) was a kind, brown-eyed North Country Protestant who was amazed and slightly shocked when I took her to Mass at Cowley.

The people I did meet through Catholicism were men. They fell into two categories – young and old, students and priests. My relationship to one fellow student – a Roman Catholic classical scholar in another college who was a lonely mother's boy like myself – did eventually grow into a lasting friendship.

When it comes to older men, the position is a bit different. The Catholics call their priests "Father," thus acknowledging the nature of the relationship. The Church, with its hierarchy of male authorities, provided me with a whole gallery of paternal substitutes.*

The first of these was the Rev. Dr. B.J. Kidd, Warden of Keble. In this case, there was a personal link with my father: they were both (literally) from the same school (Christ's Hospital), Dr. Kidd being a year or so the senior.

---

*"Substitutes" is perhaps not quite the right word here, since they did take me somehow further on my journey.

Dr. Kidd was a tall, slightly stooping, ascetic-looking person who had been a fine figure of a man in his younger days. As it was, he was exactly what my soul hankered after—my father, translated into Tractarian terms (no mean achievement, this, since my father was the most Protestant man alive). He was without my father's obtrusive potency, and was, in fact, a true father of the Church.

He was a good scholar, rather in the Pusey mould. His *History of the Church to A.D. 461* was a standard work, monumentally sound and (I imagine) monumentally dull (my discipleship, for all its enthusiasm, never drove me to the point of reading the volume). He presided in Hall regularly each night, and his tall, dark form with the white stock at the neck seemed to me the very model of a Doctor of Divinity. He used to read the lessons in Chapel, I remember, in an authoritative but unintelligible High Church mumble which used to fascinate me very much. But his walk was for me the *pièce de résistance*.

The tall, distinguished, stooping figure with the long stalking stride printed itself so vividly on my imagination as the perfection of ascetic, High Church authority that I started to imitate it myself. I couldn't become—or even want to be—a public school wallah, but I would at least picture myself as a priest. I had found a persona that really pleased me, an ego-ideal that I chose for myself, as opposed to a super-ego imposed upon me.

So I adopted the walk of a lean, ascetic priest, though my lack of faith completely excluded the ministry as a possible vocation. You may say it was a pose, and so it was (I was never a particularly serious ascetic). Yet it did perhaps correspond to a dim intuition that my true vocation might lie somewhere in the spiritual realm.

Of course, I was totally unconscious of the impression I was creating on other people. One day, as I walked along a side path in Liddon quad, one normal healthy young man remarked to another, in my hearing, "The loping priest!" The words were spoken with such concentrated contempt and disgust that I was cut to the heart with pain and shock. It was not the first time — nor was it to be the last — that I was brought up slap against the contrast between my warm, enclosed interior life and the cold secular world outside. A little corner of the blanket of illusion had been forcibly lifted, and a shaft of light came arrowing in.

Intellectually, at Oxford, I did my utmost to make the grade for Catholicism. I had conversations at St. Benet's Hall with a brilliant young Thomist philosopher, now a monk at Ampleforth and a well-known Roman Catholic writer.

One of the happiest moments in my Oxford career was part of an afternoon spent in the garden at St. Benet's with my Benedictine friend. The peace and beauty of it slid into my soul. It was at a fairly late stage in our conversations, and I remember he was talking about the ground or reason for making the act of faith: this was "the authority of God revealing," he told me. But I'm afraid that my vocational disability for Catholicism was all along that I just didn't happen to believe in God; and apparently nothing could remove my dogmatic, *a priori* incredulity.

I studied St. Thomas Aquinas' *Quinque Viae*, or five so-called Proofs of the Existence of God, in the original Latin. If I could have sold my soul to become a Catholic, I think I would have done it cheerfully. But it simply wasn't in my power: somehow, I just couldn't make it. One difficulty was the chain of infinite regression. If everything required a cause, why should God be an exception? St. Thomas makes the distinction between necessary and contingent being: *quod est non per se, est ab alio quod est per se* ("that which does not exist of itself derives its existence from something else which does exist of itself"). In a way, this is quite an impressive argument, but it didn't satisfy my simple, concrete mind — until I thought of *aseitas* ("of-itself-ness") in terms of Infinite Perfection. If God is Infinite Perfection, then he must include all other being inside himself: there can be nothing outside him to cause him.

I pretty well managed to convince myself that this was true, except that underneath I never really believed that Infinite Per-

fection could exist at all. If Infinite Perfection *did* exist, our present
universe would shrivel up in an instant in the infinite blaze of God's
blinding glory—like ice exposed to the heat of the sun.

This whole enquiry into the truth of Christianity was of very
real concern to me. It involved the deeper layers of the personality. The effort I put out in thinking seems to have stirred the unconscious into motion.

One day at Bedford during the vacation I found myself spontaneously composing a poem. On the whole I was still far too
divided by neurosis to be able to write effectively. But the fact
that this poem did crystallise out suggests that, without my knowing it, my intellectual and emotional searching had exerted some
unifying effect on me.

The verse was quite traditional—in the Tennysonian style—
and I called it "Enigma," and (later) "Quest."

I do not know
What power spins the stars in ceaseless flight,
Or why, like pilgrim to eternal snow,
Life strives towards the height;
Yet this I know:
Somewhere far down the reaches of the night
The silver lamp of truth is burning slow,
Burning with flame of white.

I was forced finally to leave my quest without an answer. It got
shelved somewhere on the lower strata of the psyche. And yet the
point remained at issue, and therefore potentially liable to re-
emerge in a later chapter of the story.

My father Eugene Alfred Rolfe in his later years.

My mother Rose Emily Sansom shortly before she was married.

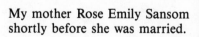

My mother holding me
at my christening.

Photo of Eugene 1917,
captioned: "My darling
boy at the age of 3
years, when he was very
like his mother"

Eugene, age 11, and
Joan Rolfe in garden at
7 St Andrew's Road,
Bedford.

At Miss Beall's
Preparatory School,
July 1922.

II

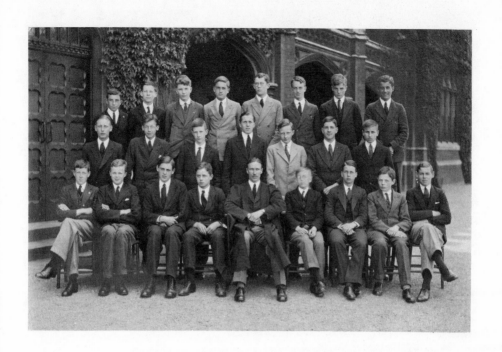

Bedford School—With Mr. Boys-
Stoner in the Vth form. Eugene
seated second from right.

Eugene Rolfe in the Liddon Quad
at Keble College, 1935

III

Eugene and Ilse Rolfe celebrating their 40th Anniversary.

Daughter Marlene Rolfe.

Eugene Rolfe with his favorite cat and "co-editor" Pussymum.

IV

IV
Rome _____

I particularly admired the exotic flowering shrubs —
laburnum, may, lilac, etc.— which make North Oxford into
a Mediterranean garden of spices for a few brief weeks during the spring. All this I associated with the spicy ritual
and incense-laden worship of the Latin Church; it was part of
the background of the cult. There is very little doubt in my mind
that it had absorbed as well as superseded the worship of the old
Mediterranean Mother-goddess.

The priests of Cybele in their frenzied adoration used to con-
summate the final ecstasy of union with the *Magna Mater* by cutting off the male organ of generation. They literally enacted the
fantasy of castration which is the appointed punishment for incest with the Mother. Though I always, at the back of my mind,
somehow hoped to get married, in practice my own mother-
involvement had placed me in a not dissimilar position. My fantasies of myself as an ascetic priest fit in perfectly well with this

19

pattern.

For the majority of the faithful, who are leading a more or less normal family life, the Catholic system, with its firm and durable faith and morals, its calendrical cycle linked to the seasons, and its rites and sacraments that elicit the meaning of the great climacteric occasions of life, does amount to something like a preventive health-service for the psyche, with comprehensive coverage from the cradle to the grave. At the hub of this wheel stands the ritual of the Mass — and this was my own point of contact with the system. It is the duty of every Catholic to attend mass on Sundays, an obligation which dates back to the origins of Christianity. Though I was a fellow-traveller, not a practising Catholic, I did get this particular obligation pretty deeply lodged in my nervous system. Since that time I have rarely missed a week, and to this day I should feel distinctly uneasy if I had not managed to attend the Eucharist or its equivalent on a Sunday.

As it happened, this habit of attendance at the Eucharist turned out to be my one permanent link with organised Christianity. It meant a tremendous amount to me; and yet I couldn't explain why. So another aspect of my unsolved religious problem was filed in the "pending" tray of the unconscious.

V
Harley Street _____

I have to admit it: those years at Oxford were in many ways the most satisfying period of my life. Yet the *libido sexualis* once aroused by masturbation was still suppressed and unsatisfied. My ruling system of ideas left me no way of understanding or resolving this problem. I still had to wage a running war against acute, obsessional anxiety-doubt; the distraint on my energy was so severe that I failed to put in the solid work required for the First in (Classical) Mods. which was expected of me.

When, in 1935, I took a good Second, and the anxiety seemed just as acute as ever. I was stung into one of my periodic attempts to do something about it. I appealed to my old mentors, the Pelman people. Finally they gave me the name and address of Dr. William Brown, of 88 Harley Street. I wrote to him at once, describing my symptoms. He replied, and diagnosed my trouble as a case of "anxiety hysteria."

This gave me that exquisite sensation of relief—one of the most poignant pleasures in the world—of having a name put to an unknown torment. You imagine that, alone among mankind, you are smitten by some ghastly, unique affliction; and behold! The condition falls into a medical category: thousands if not millions of your fellow-mortals are afflicted with the same malady.

This was a generation before the time of university or college psychiatric services. Fortunately for me, however, a portion of one of my grants for the University happened to be at my own disposal; so that I was actually able to consult Dr. William Brown with a view to some treatment.

Dr. Brown—tall, red-faced, an establishment figure, with an unaccountable streak of the old woman about him—received me in his lofty Georgian consulting-room. I must say, he was agreeably frank. He didn't attempt to conceal from me the fact that analysis was in his opinion the only radical cure for my trouble. As I was an Oxford undergraduate, and he was the Wilde Reader in Mental Philosophy at the University, he was willing to treat me at his specially reduced rate of two guineas an hour (as against the normal five guineas). At that rate, my disposable funds would make exactly nine hours' treatment possible for me.

He told me (again, with engaging candour) that Freud did not approve of suggestion-treatment at all, but that he (Dr. Brown) found it helpful in certain cases. Not unnaturally in the circumstances, I plumped for suggestion.

The procedure was as follows. I used to lie down on a couch, and when I was sufficiently dozy Dr. Brown would repeat over me at intervals certain formulae, of which the following fragments have remained imprinted on my mind: "Quite passive, quite relaxed, learn things well, remember things well, thoroughly fit and well and strong, quite passive, quite relaxed thoroughly fit and well and strong, learn things well, remember things well, RELAX, RELAX, RELAX."

The formulae used to go round and round, in a kind of incantatory sing-song, until, after the prayer-wheel had been revolving for two or three minutes, Dr. Brown used to remove himself some distance behind a screen, where he made a mysterious crinkly noise, apparently with some newspapers. To this day, I've never managed to find out what he was doing with those papers. After that he'd come back, and the wheel of persuasion would start revolving again. After four or five recurrences of this performance, I'd dish out my guineas and be gone.

This treatment was a palliative, not a cure. Yet it had a decisive effect on my life. It poured oil on the troubled waters, and soothed me and smoothed me down to such an extent that I was able to complete my University studies. Whichever way you look at it, the class I managed to take in "Greats" is a testimonial I'd gladly sign to the benefit of Dr. Brown's suggestive capsules!

The position of my mind during those Oxford years was that — like most of my contemporaries — I'd heard about the Big Three (Freud, Jung and Adler) but that — like most people, again — I identified psychology with the depth analysis introduced by this triumvirate; experimental psychology was beyond our purview.

I had read Freud's *Interpretation of Dreams*. The intricacies of Freud's argument — the manifest dream thought, the latent dream thought, the dream work, and so on — I found quite tough and difficult to understand, but I believed that what Freud said was essentially true, just as I believed that what Dr. Brown said was true. It came to me with the authority of medical science, and though this may not actually have been "the authority of God revealing," it came with a not altogether dissimilar compulsion.

Typically, again, I had read no Jung; but this didn't prevent me from having an opinion about him that was both definite and adverse. I'd heard somewhere that he believed in free will. This, to my mind, disposed of him. Quite obviously, he had not thought the subject through! Later (again, like most of my contemporaries) I read Jung's *Modern Man in Search of a Soul*. The book made no impression on me that I can remember.

I attended the lectures which Dr. Brown (in his capacity as Wilde Reader) gave in Christ Church Hall. The unforgettable climax of

the series came on the morning when Dr. Brown introduced no
less a personage than the great Alfred Adler himself.

I remember him as dumpy, sympathetic, central European, Jewish, with a wealth of expansive gesticulation. But what really
knocked me backwards about him was that he was so radiantly
and shiningly social-minded — positive, friendly and
constructive — so obviously on the side of the angels. I'd been conditioned by the atmosphere which seemed to emanate from Freud
(and the Freudian school) to take it completely as a matter of
course that depth psychology *must* necessarily be profoundly subversive of morality and social order. Yet Adler (incidentally the
only one of the Big Three who was an active, professing Social
Democrat) was refreshingly immune from this tendency.

I remember Dr. Brown addressing him and saying, "Dr. Adler,
we in England have all heard about the three great names in
psychology — Freud, Jung, and Adler. Now, it would interest us
very much to know, what do you think of *Freud?*"

"Ah, Freud!" Dr. Adler replied, throwing out his hands in front
of him with the palms extended outwards in a characteristic ges-
ture, "We theenk he is LOFFLEE!"

The only other thing I can remember about Adler's lecture was
a remark of his which seemed to me to have a dark and cryptic
boding force: "When the possibility of success disappears, the possibility of death appears." This principle had already been exemplified in my own life, when my failure to conquer masturbation
had been followed by my attempts to kill myself.

VI
A Career? _____

My "class" provided one vocational hint: verbal aptitude. Characteristically I didn't take it. The field of vocational alternatives had been preselected for me by my father's academic milieu. The door to the Church was closed to me by my lack of faith. I couldn't teach in a school. I'd never thought about the law or medicine — still less the armed forces. What remained was the civil service.

I'd arrived at a perfectly "suitable" choice without once consulting my inclination! The world of culture and religion, to which my whole heart and mind belonged, had been left on one side without a word of protest. It was an astonishing defeat for my personality. It shows how at this climacteric moment, when the tracks ran out over the crossing into life, the power of positive selection had been simply lifted out of my hands.

I took the Civil Service "Admin." exam shortly after "Greats," and in the middle of a nervous breakdown. No doubt the two of them in succession were just a bit too much. Almost literally, I couldn't write. I kept writing words and crossing them out. I was getting marks in the region of seventeen out of a hundred. The solitary exceptions were the Latin Unseen (inside the area energised by the mother-passion for Catholicism), for which I was given eighty-six out of a hundred; and, of all things, the personality test (interview), for which I got the full three hundred out of three hundred marks!

There's a story behind this astonishing reversal of form at the interview. To begin with, my mother came up from Bedford and gave me a tot of brandy before I went in. I'd got to the stage when I was simply incapable of worrying any more about what happened. In a sense, nothing was at stake; and the brandy simply lifted the lid off and released my uninhibited self, so that, for once, I was able to be spontaneous and natural.

The woman member of the Broad happened to be Lady Violet Bonham-Carter. I remember her sympathetic brown eyes — she made me feel entirely at home. She asked me the subject of the essay I had read at Keble. I told her "The Defence of the Feminine." Possibly this didn't make a bad impression; but she went on to ask me if I was acquainted with the work of Arthur Whaley. Now, it just so happened I'd recently bought a second-hand copy of *More Translations from the Chinese* at Blackwell's. So we had an interesting little talk about masculine and feminine characters in Chinese poetry. What could possibly be further removed from the business of public administration! Yet what could be nearer to my own essential interests!

So long as I had some positive link with the feminine — my own mother, the brandy, Lady Vi, and the Chinese verses — I was all right. I was an example, on a microscopic scale, of the classical motif of Antaeus and Gaea. The fact remains that in the total examination order my place was number 150!

My mother now entered the field for the second time. Characteristically, she appealed to the Prime Minister. It was no less typical of her that her appeal was actually successful. Mr. Baldwin asked me to come and see him at his London home in Eaton Square.

My old hero-worship (this, of course, had been my mother's main plank) had unfortunately evaporated by this time, though I naturally didn't draw attention to this fact at the interview.

I noticed two things about Stanley Baldwin. One was the rugged strength of his face — bristling eyebrows, craggy jaw. This was certainly not the weak vacillator, blown about by every wind, who appeared in the Press Peers' caricature image of him. He was suffering severely from gout, and when he walked he leaned heavily on a stick. And that brings me to the second point. I noticed, when the time came for him to show me out, that he used stick and gait to dramatise his ailment. He put on a little act for my benefit. I was disappointed. Mentally, I awarded him a debit mark (though I did not pause to consider the possible existence of a similar tendency in my humble self).

But defects have their qualities, too. And it was with the greatest interest that — something like twenty-five years later — I read the following pertinent comment on him by no less an authority than A. J. P. Taylor: "Baldwin was really a remarkable actor."[*]

He was certainly one of the two or three most effective broadcasters of the inter-war period (in this respect, I would bracket him with G. K. Chesterton). And he managed to put across his preferred persona of English pipe-smoking trustworthiness and fair play with quite astonishing success.

When I left, he remarked that I hadn't got a hat. I told him I hadn't worn one since leaving school. He accepted this with a good-humoured smile. The net result of my mother's intervention was a grant of £200, to enable me to study for another year and take the Admin. exam a second time.

I lived at home and read without much enthusiasm. But a year which might have been stagnant, if not regressive, was enlivened by one new positive development.

My worries (now in the shape of compulsive symptoms) were

*See "The Baldwin Years" in *The Listener,* 15th March, 1962.

still dogging me pretty close. This time they drove me to the point
of attending the Out-Patients' Clinic for Nervous Disorders at the
Bedford County Hospital. A little Greek doctor who saw me there
dropped one really invaluable suggestion, like a pearl into my out-
stretched palm. He told me it would be good for me to take up
swimming.

I took lessons, and after some time I succeeded in learning a
rather rudimentary kind of crawl. Later, at Cambridge, I improved
the crawl slightly and added the breast-stroke, which I found a
bit easier.

The exercise was splendid in every way. In the first place, each
time before I went round to the baths I had to struggle against
my own resistance — which was painful, but exactly the medicine
I needed. And the actual swimming brought a release of motor
and athletic impulses which had been blocked up in me as a boy,
and also a delicious, primitive sensual pleasure which I'd certainly
never experienced before. It was a body-builder combined with
an erotic outlet — at one and the same time both the chastest and
the most sensual of sports. And it is about as far away from anxiety as modern sophisticated man is likely to get.

My work in the Admin. Exam. of '38 was uninspired but steady.
I came 102nd in the Examination Order. I was twenty four years
old; and now, for the first time in my life, I was faced with the
world at large as it exists outside the precincts of St. Scholastica.

I badly needed guidance, so I went to the National Institute
of Industrial Psychology and had a Vocational Guidance Consultation. The N.I.I.P gave me a personal interview and put me
through a selection from their own battery of tests. I remember
that the able and handsome young doctor who saw me (he looked
rather like Robert Donat) remarked on my awkwardness at the
end of an interview. In his report, he came down in favour of
a Museum appointment, an L.C.C. or Civil Service type post, and
librarianship, in that order.

I decided to try for the museum job. Some knowledge of
German — at least a "librarian's smattering," I was told — was es-

sential for the post. As I had none — I didn't even know the meaning of *Sitten* (morals) in Immanuel Kant's philosophical writings — I bought a paperback *Hugo's German Grammar Simplified* and began to study.

At the same time, I did feel very strongly that something would have to be done about me personally before I really set out to work in the world. Through my father's Brighton friend (the one who had taken us to church at St. Martin's), I got to hear about Father John Maillard, the Anglican faith healer. I wrote to him, and arranged to spend two weeks at his healing centre at Milton Abbey, near Blandford, in Dorset.

I could afford to pay for this period, but when it was over I stayed on at Father Maillard's invitation, and it wasn't until April, 1939 (six months later) that I left.

I'd explained to Father Maillard quite frankly at the outset that I was an agnostic. However, he stoutly maintained his conviction that faith on the part of the patient himself was not always essential; the prayers of other people might also act as the channel for Divine Healing. I received the laying-on of hands with prayer on a number of occasions. I certainly didn't shut my mind against anything; but obviously, my lack of vital positive faith must have been a factor affecting at least my own outlook. And I can only say that I experienced no spectacular (let alone miraculous) cure through this channel.

Yet I did benefit from my stay at Milton Abbey, though the healing I actually received was something more subtle, more diffuse, far less spectacular, yet no less "Christian" than a so-called "miracle of faith." It came from the natural and social environment of the place.

The magnificent decorated Abbey Church and the eighteenth century mansion, built, like a college, round a hollow square, stood on their own grounds — nine hundred acres of them. Between the Abbey and the village of Milton Abbas lay a valley — a *mire vallis* (wonderful valley) I called it, since it reminded me irresistibly of the ancient title which the Cistercians gave to one of their English houses — Merevale, at Atherstone.

This secluded paradise, with its small stream (called, with na-ive aptness, the Piddle), its Monk's Walk, its grass steps, and its St. Catharine's Chapel crowning their steep spectacular flight, formed a marvelous, romantic, natural setting. Milton Abbey might have been shaped for the express purpose of receiving the projection of my wild monastic unconscious. I love the place, and honestly didn't want to leave it — though I kept on with my Ger-man studies.

On the human side, the Abbey was a remarkable community; its members came from the most variegated tribal habitats, both socially and ecclesiastically high and low. But the whole conger-ies was welded into what can only be — and was — called a family by their common interest in faith-healing and their common de-votion to Father Maillard ("Father").

Some of us patients used to do rhythmic exercises to music in the open (I was told Father Maillard believed in combining pray-er with physical motion). There was also simple work for us such as carting wood. On some evenings, there were sing-song recitals; there were also regular dances.

This Abbey Family was a couple of decades ahead of its time in its approach to mental disorder. Through a creative applica-tion of the Christian family concept, it had in effect arrived at that "healing through community" (in contrast to the old quarantine-in-asylum system), which is just now coming into its own in England as the preferred environment for mental treatment.

Father Maillard himself was a tall, big-boned, red-blooded man — the ideal father for such a family. When he entered the room, the temperature of morale would leap up by twenty degrees or so. He had begun as an East End Anglo-Catholic priest. So-cially and culturally, he was not absolutely out of the top drawer. This was more unusual than it is now among the ministers of the established Church, and it set him free from some of the inhibi-tions which restricted the old "gentleman-in-every-parish" caste. He used to drive a Hudson Straight-Eight; and when I needed to go to London, he motored me up from Dorset to Bayswater (where the Healing Mission had a chapel) at a speed which alarmed me by touching eighty in places.

The effect of the Milton Abbey mixture upon me — good food, fresh air, reasonable exercise, the enchanted valley and the warm, human familial atmosphere — is best gauged by the simple fact that after six months or so of it I was ready to sally forth into the workaday world.

The British Museum job didn't come along. I had an interview for it, but was rejected, apparently because of my lack of German — paradoxically, the one modern language I was later able to speak and write fluently. Instead, the L.C.C. made me a proposal; and after another interview, I was offered the post of First Class 'B' Assistant (approximately equivalent to Assistant Principal in the Civil Service). As may be imagined, I was desperately anxious to get started in the world, and the obvious course was to accept this position.

There was, however, one unfortunate snag which worried me a great deal. One of the questions on the form I had to sign ran "Have you ever suffered from any form of nervousness or nervous trouble?" To answer "No" would be incorrect; to answer "Yes" would be to destroy my chances. My psychological history was dogging me here, very much like a prison record.

In this dilemma, I applied to Father Maillard, who was my authority-figure at the time. I remember speaking to him in a window embrasure along one of the corridors which ran round the sides of the Milton Abbey quadrangle. The tall, red-blooded, stout-boned figure, in the fatherly cassock with the wavy shoulder-hood that added to the virile priest just that soupçon of the maternal — Father Maillard was there protectingly beside me. He was supercharged with vitality and optimism.

I showed him the offending question. His reply was unhesitating and decisive: "My dear boy," he told me, "You've *never* suffered from nervousness. Write NIL NIL NIL!"

The gave me the encouragement I needed, and I made the leap

I could never have dared by myself. I duly wrote "NIL NIL NIL," got the job in the L.C.C., and started work in the Public Assistance Department (Area VII: Battersea, Lambeth and Wandsworth) in May, 1939.

There is an incident in the Gospel which is not printed in the received text, though it occurs in one good manuscript (the Codex Bezae) after Luke VI, "On the same day, he saw someone working on the Sabbath and said to him, 'If you know what you're doing, you are blessed; but if you don't know, you are accursed and a transgressor of the law'."

This is a very clear statement about levels of ethical maturity. The man who has discovered his own inner path may—and indeed must—on occasion disregard the letter, the collective convention, of morality. But the man who is still *in statu pupillari* (not yet of age) and dependent, as it were, on the external ordinances carved upon the tablets of stone, will disregard their warning at his peril. For him, truth is still projected on the literal formulations of the moral law; if he breaks these, he will be a transgressor.

Father Maillard himself knew how urgently necessary it was for me to come right out into the world and confront life on my own feet. So he used his preponderating influence to help me to overcome my scruples.

I myself was still very much *in statu pupillari*. Though I had the courage to accept Father Maillard's advice, I never felt happy about it underneath. And as long as I remained in the dependent stage, there was always the possibility that a day of reckoning might overtake me—for example, another "father" might appear who would annul the comfortable words Father Maillard had spoken.

VII
Analysis! _____

For the first time in my life (and I was twenty five), I now had an income of my own. I soon put my name down for treatment (at reduced rates) at the Tavistock Clinic; and on 13th November, 1939, I started analysis. I had three hours a week pretty continuously till I left London in October, 1940. The charge was 7 pounds 6 pence an hour.

I was warned at the outset not to do two things during the course of the treatment: change my job or get married. As it happened, I managed to do both before I was finished with one sort of analysis or another! Yet I didn't contravene the wishes of my analyst in either case.

The treatment was on moderate Freudian lines. I called up all the memories I could of my childhood situation, as far back as possible — attraction to mother, fear of father, guilt, etc. I could remember a series of little incidents that had stuck like snapshots in my memory; put together, they pinpointed the Oedipus situation very clearly.

As the outbreak of war, I'd managed to talk myself into pacifism — "there is no situation in which war is justified." If I had had to register then, I would have put myself down as a conscientious objector. I had stand-up fights with my analyst about this, and in the end he did compel me to see that pacifism was an escape from life, a desire to protect myself at all costs. Underneath my surface moral rationalisation, I felt quite simply, in a resentful way, that the country hadn't allowed me to possess a woman, and so I was damned if I was going to fight and die for it — a projection of my mother-complex upon England, no doubt.*

I'd really been waiting for this analysis since I met Dr. Brown in 1935; I went in for it in a great wave of religious faith. Catholicism provided me with an emotional anchorage and a scale of prejudices and values; but this was *faith* — the same utter, unquestioning confidence that men had given to the Church perhaps six centuries earlier. It didn't occur to me for a moment that any other schools or techniques of therapy might be worthy of consideration. In this respect, I was a typical English intellectual of the thirties.

Before I was finished with the Tavistock Clinic, I'd received, by the way, a good deal of instruction in the theory of psychoanalysis, so that concepts like the unconscious, the ego, the superego, the id, repression, "reality," etc., became familiar parts of my mental furniture. But it was not simply a matter of indoctrination. The ideas were related to real elements in my personality and life-situation. And I was able to do some original work.

For instance, one morning as I lay in bed, I was puzzling over the irrational terror I had of dogs — and railway engines — as a small child. Suddenly, it flashed into my mind that the dog was a substitute object for my buried fear of my own father. This was a genuine discovery, which came home to me with convincing force.

---

*I *don't* say that all pacifism, as such, is intrinsically escapist. I *do* say that my pacifism, at that stage, was an evasion of life.

I remember being described at the clinic as a case of "suppressed aggression." This was true enough. I realised later that I was (both physically and temperamentally) a tender-skin, so that there was a constitutional basis as well as an early conditioning behind my mild and milky manners. Another point which only dawned on me later was that my middle-class Christian milieu, in which aggression was at a total discount, played into the hands of the neurosis all along.

Yet assertive and fighting instincts did exist, though driven deep down below the surface. If they hadn't, there would of course have been no problem.

VIII
Resign! Resign! _____

My first analyst, a young English doctor, was eventually called up into the Navy (this was something like six months after the beginning of the war). His successor was an older man—a distinguished émigré from Germany with a Heidelberg degree (he had actually been the supervisor of analyst number one. His name was Dr. Koenigsberger).

Among other things, I told him about my feelings of guilt at having stated on the L.C.C. entrance form that I had never suffered from any form of nervousness or nervous trouble. He said, "In my country, we would have called that 'opportunism'!"

This brought my feelings of anxiety to the surface in a really intolerable form. Authority had allied itself with my scruples. I imagine my analyst did this quite deliberately. He was fully capable of handling the situation, and we should no doubt have worked through this complication together. But unfortunately, at this

moment, he went sick! I was left high and dry on the horns of
my dilemma.

I expostulated to the clinic as well as I was able, and insisted
that I really must see somebody. And after a bit, I got a third
analyst. This time it was a woman—a Scot; her name was Dr.
Lilley, and I can honestly say, she was one of the best I have had,
in a lengthy and not altogether unvariegated experience.

By now, I was bursting with desire to resign from the L.C.C.
But I remembered the warning I had been given, and held firmly
on to the principle of at any rate not doing anything *against* my
analyst. We discussed the question up and down. She didn't conceal from me her opinion that the root cause of my difficulty was
the acute anxiety I felt at the prospect of taking up my "masculine entitlement." But she had also come to the conclusion that
I wasn't really in the right job. So, though she didn't give me any
definite vocational advice, she didn't oppose my own wishes, either.
Finally she told me, "Well, Mr. Rolfe, you'll have to go your own
way!"

Authority had now given me permission to resign; so resign I
did. I wrote in a long letter to headquarters, telling my story and
giving my reasons. It was a very carefully-drafted paper—the best
bit of work, I daresay, that I ever did for the London County
Council!

Like my entry into its service, my resignation from the L.C.C.
was a climacteric moment in my history. At the time, the war was
on and the employment situation was exceedingly fluid. But as
the long run of years was to show, I had in effect divested myself
of my university qualifications, stripped off the armour-plating
of difference hung around me by my privileged education, and
flung myself upon the mercies of the open market.

I fled from London two or three weeks after the Blitz settled
in, and for the last fortnight of my L.C.C. career I came up daily
from the old home in Bedford. I felt no duty towards London,
since I had no emotional link with it and no sense of belonging
to it. It sounds bad, but it's the truth. Objectively, I could see

what a fine service the L.C.C. was in many ways. Subjectively, I loathed it as a child might loathe an alien guardian standing in its light. I was in fact in the wrong job.

Still, I did feel bad about running away; and I talked this over with my analyst. She told me very wisely that there are some stages and situations where you just had to act in this way. The fact is that, in spite of my spurts of courage, I was still an appallingly frightened person. I think the wisdom of the decision was justified by the event.

I had five months' unemployment in Bedford before I took up my next job. I visibly revived, like a wilting flower which has been put back into the nourishing earth. The link with the Mother was restored.

After a while, I even wrote a letter to the *Bedfordshire Times,* descanting in glowing colours on the glorious heritage of our medieval system of strip cultivation of the common fields. The theme was not quite so maniacally escapist as it sounds, since those were the days when "Common Wealth" and similar movements were drawing up visionary blue-prints of the new England that was to be created after the war. The letter was bursting with renewed vitality.

I'd masturbated once or twice, and this scared me very much. Now my anxiety drove me to the point of going out to look for a woman. I'd done this before in London (after the analysis had started); but my longings and prowlings had all come to nothing.

Now, one evening, as I walked abroad, I saw a girl standing by the door of the café that formed part of the Granada Cinema in St. Peter's Street, Bedford. She was holding on to the handle of the door, and seemed to be feeling ill.

I walked away, and then back again, and struggled — unbelievably hard — with myself. If she had not been apparently in need of help, I would never have dared to speak to her: it was the old damsel in distress motif which gave me the courage and the moral pretext I needed to spike the guns of my overwhelming Christian reluctance to making any kind of sexual approach to a woman.

Eventually, I stood up alongside of her, as it were, and said, rather formally, "Good evening!" She looked at me, there was a slight pause, and then she started talking. I walked back with her to Kempston, where she was living, a mile-and-a-half or so away. She told me that she had just felt a bit sick, and had clung to the café doorhandle for support.

I met her several times after that; but my inhibitions returned after the initial break-through, and all I could manage was some rather lame, juvenile conversation. She was a French girl, as it happened, dark and rather wellformed. Her name was Josette — which I, for Freudian reasons, kept forgetting and replacing by "Rosette" — and she came from Bourges, in the centre of France.

One evening, at Kempston, as I was saying goodnight and standing there up against her, feeling awkward, she reached up towards my face and made a little pecking movement, like a bird. So the first time I kissed a girl was the first time a girl kissed me!

I remember another occasion, also at Kempston, when we were sitting side by side in a green field which sloped down to the river Ouse, just opposite the barracks of the Beds. and Herts. Regiment. Something annoyed me, and I actually showed some signs of temper — instead of my usual meek, lamb-like approach. "I like you much better like this," she said.

The relationship came to an end when I went back to London to a new job. I wrote her a letter in a poetic, imaginative vein, with bits about priests incanting the sad, dull tone of the dead which may well have been new to her — although she was a Roman Catholic!

This slight little affair marked a colossal leap forwards for me. It was a decisive advance towards liberation. Without the gruelling hours spent confessing in analysis, it would — and could — never have happened. But the strange thing was that it happened at *Bedford,* where all my original inhibitions had been laid down, and where every kind of traditional restraint was, as it were, laden in the atmosphere. In going home to Bedford, I had found

my way back to the nourishing Mother, and the springs of life
had gushed forth from her breast.

As before at Milton Abbey, I found that after five or six months,
these healing streams had so far restored me that I was ready to
sally forth into the world again. I got a job as a temporary clerk
in the Fire Brigades Division of the Home Office. I returned to
London in time for the last two big raids of the Blitz. In one of
these, Horseferry House, the office block where I had been working during the day, was hit during the night.

With intervals, my analysis continued. I think that this form
of treatment was possibly the finest moral discipline I have even
been subjected to in my life. Freud had said *"Alles sagen ist wirk-
lich alles sagen,"* and the technique of free association did actually mean that you had to try to say *literally* everything that came
into your head. It reached the point, for example, when you had
to speculate about the colour of your woman analyst's pubic hair!
For those inside the antiseptic circle of medicine (psychological
medicine), this, no doubt, is a trivial detail of diurnal routine.
But to anyone who had been brought up under the full rigour
of the Protestant bourgeois reticence about sex, it really was a
crucial test!

Outside the analytical hour, the discipline was equally strenu-
ous. For several years I really did make the most sacrificial efforts
to break down my inhibitions. Very slowly, within limits, I had
some success — but it was a terrible uphill struggle, since the enemy was entrenched in my own psyche. It was almost like unpick-
ing a suit of clothes that had grown into your own skin.

Now, as I look back after forty years, I can see that the awful
congestion, constriction and clotted mess of guilt that thickened
and tramelled my neurotic chest has largely lifted and cleared away.

On Good Friday, 1941, I made my only serious attempt to write
a poem in the modern manner. It is a shade longer than my previous efforts, seven years earlier, in the Tennysonian vein.

Draw me forwards into the flowing,

Merge me with the stream,
Dissolving the clutching fingers of my resistance:
Let me be carried.
No more flagellation, no more fever
Slashing aslant the movement of time,
But a uniform procession downstream,
In which endeavour shall be only the flowering of motion,
The green tips spurting at the front of a million years.

I called this poem "Surrender."

That year, the time came for me to register for military service; I did so in the ordinary way. I had completely given up the idea of pacifism. All the same, my woman analyst sent a note to the Medical Board, which put them in the picture about the slightly mottled state of my psyche. As a result, I was put in Grade IV, which meant that, for practical purposes, I was exempt from military service.

IX
The Factory _____

In the meantime, a great change and shift of interest was simmering and brewing away in the unconscious. I became dissatisfied with my work as a temporary clerk; I wanted to do something more physical.

One idea was to work on the land. I wanted to do it — my love-life lay there, the same Lilliput Antaeus still straining backwards to reach his Gaea — but the whole subject was far too heavily laden with guilt. Once again I collided head-on with the adamantine barrier against incest with the Mother. It was as if the Commander-in-Chief of the Unconscious (a matriarch, of course) had issued me with the First and Great Commandment: Thou shalt not follow thy inclination!

Fortunately for me, another opportunity came along: I got a job as a process-worker grade III in Royal Ordnance Factory No. 19 at Elstow, some three miles south of Bedford. I worked there for fifteen months.

The business of the factory was filling. It filled shells for light mortars and 7.2mm naval defence guns, and it filled 4,000 lb. blockbuster bombs. We ourselves—the little party I was with—worked with ammonium nitrate, a substance like artificial snow.

Our task was to "stem" this snowy substance down into powder and fragments, using for this purpose upright beams that for some reason reminded me of pew-ends. It was then filtered through a grille in the floor to the boiler in the shop underneath. I found the work satisfying, and not too taxing. It gave my meagre, unused, girlish arms some very badly-needed development.

On the whole, I got on surprisingly well with my fellow-workers. Their picaresque attitude to sex was a completely new and delightful revelation to me. The depleted state of the unfortunate human male after the (possibly repeated) performance of his sexual offices was a matter of rueful humour, shared in common, not for ghastly anxiety hugged in solitude.

One old Bedfordshire worker called Ernie had a quite special personal appeal for me. He was 73 (a few months older than my father), and came from Clophill, on the greensand ridge. He was a wonderfully hale old man, really, though at the same time there was something diminutive and tortoise-like about him. He used to tell me about his sexual exploits. I asked him when he first began to go after women, and he answered, "Oh! as soon as I got my ink!" From what I know about Ernie, I should say this was likely enough. But the idea that this vital bodily fluid might be linked, just so soon as it became available, directly to the object for which it was by nature intended still seemed, to the middle-class Puritan inside me, an outrageous and barely conceivable paradox.

There was a twinkle and a sly cunning about Ernie which made him an ideal counter-heroic figure—if you like, he was the Sancho Panza to my father's Don Quixote. I can't remember Ernie without affection—and I certainly cannot, and will not, forget him.

The mural epigraphy in the men's lavatories at times achieved classic status. The one bit that has remained embedded in my memory came straight out of the well-fount of English folk-poetry:

> Apples are red,
> Nuts are brown.
> Petticoats up,
> Trousers down.

I learned a lot in that factory. From the social point of view, it was my initiation into the working life of the 80% of the English population from which I'd been cut off by my middle-class upbringing.

But of course, the social class which is excluded by your own social class corresponds to the tabooed elements in your own personality. That this is a general principle — that it does, in fact, work both ways — is proved by such a novel as *Room at the Top*. In my own case, the part cut off was obviously the genitals and the whole animal life of sex. It was the permissiveness of my analysis at Tavistock which had provided me with the key that unlocked this door.

My woman analyst had been slightly irritated and quite openly incredulous when I told her that I didn't know the English vernacular word for the vagina. Yet this was literally the case. When she told me the word I rummaged in my memory, and suddenly a line from Chaucer came into my mind: "He caught her privily by the quaint."

So the middle-class English intellectual had to go back to the *Canterbury Tales* to discover the word that is written up on the walls of practically every male public lavatory in the country!

X
My Father's Death _____

uring the time I was at Chimney Corner, my father died. He was in his seventy-third year, and was fit and potent right up to the last; he could play a respectable game of tennis when he was over seventy.

He had, I think, been slightly shocked when I used to come home from the factory and smoke a Woodbine in front of the dining-room fire. But he'd been amused by what I told him about Ernie, and this saving sense of humour seems to me almost symbolic — as if a reconciliation is possible after all between these two figures and the worlds apart for which they stood.

His death was a tremendous blow to me — it struck home, right to the heart. All my buried sympathy for him came rushing to the surface, and I knew that in some way I was called to be his successor (I was the only male member of our little family).

Physically and personally, I'm afraid I just hadn't got the stuffing to be the man my father was. All the same, for six months

47

after his death the wages I brought home from the factory were the only money coming into the house.

Culturally, I did stand in my father's tradition; in a sense it was true to say (as I told him) that I believed in all the things he believed in. Have we any right (I wonder) to just totally reject the cultural inheritance left us by our parents? I personally doubt it — unless (most exceptionally) this inheritance happens to be entirely vile. What they leave us might be compared to the spiritual genes out of which we construct out own vital fabric. But in my case, there was never any question about it.

What I received from my father was the water I swam in, the air I breathed, my home, my faith, my element — easily the most important non-physical influence in my life. The image of the jealous, disciplinarian father which had come up in my analysis at the Tavistock was all right as far as it went — provided you remember he also had a kind, fatherly, loving side. But my father had another role which ran clean out beyond the personal.

He had been the agent, the splendid representative, the priestly mediator between myself and the great central tradition of culture through which man had developed into the modern world. Even my outsize mother-passion for Catholicism was accommodated within the paternal edifice. In my father's house were many rooms. I might still be living in the same house long after all personal complexes had been forgotten.

During my time at Chimney Corner, I had started learning German again. I'd done enough in my first bout of study to convince myself that I quite liked the language. But in those days, at Milton Abbey, in 1938, the star of Catholicism was still glowing triumphantly in the ascendant. Since then, the analysis had gone to work and caused quite a shift in the alignment of the unconscious. The time was ripe for the emergence of a new constellation.

I remember musing as I walked a long the cleanways at the factory over a fragment of composition that was meant to be the end-piece of a book. It was headed *Nox et tenebrae et nubila* (Night And Darkness And Clouds).

Nox et tenebrae et nubila
   The cycles shift and swing, and as the focus settles, I see a priest of the old order. He comes in vested to the altar, and begins his Mass. In the midst of the stillness two tapers glimmer, like stars through the September gloom. *Introibo ad altare Dei: ad Deum qui laetificat juventutem meam.** The voice continues, and round me I can feel all human beings that ever drew breath pressing forwards through the darkness and joining their voices with the murmured insistency of the priest. Suddenly there is a burst of unearthly, tumultuous song. Beyond sorrow, beyond pain, beyond the weariness of living, in deep-throated unison the voices rise and swell, chanting the great Credo of the human spirit. As last the music fades, dying on the note of uplifted victory and calm. The colours swirl, and I can only see two tapers burning in a mist.
   When I look again, the world is very cold. With silent mysterious glide vapours pass in procession over the face of the night sky. Stars appear and reappear, faint points through the drift. The earth, untenanted, rolls onwards through the dark.

The first thing that strikes me when I read this epilogue today is its overwhelmingly traditional style. It reminds me of Froude's celebrated passage about the Middle Ages, which I loved and used to know by heart.

But behind the style there is a "real" experience, something of a visual character that I'd seen or glimpsed. I'm not claiming (or disclaiming) any particular metaphysical status for this. You can call it a fantasy if you like: it was certainly related to the imagination. But in that case the genus "fantasy" will really need to be divided into at least two subordinate species, since this item was altogether different in quality from anything I'd thrown up in analysis at Tavistock. It was somehow more objective and solid, and very much less personal.

In this respect, it's rather like "Surrender"; but unlike "Surrender," its vestments are unmistakably Catholic. It is really a kind of agnostic apocalypse of humanity, in which the unity of our race is expressed in a corporate paean of affirmation, which then

---

*I will go unto the altar of God: ever unto the God that maketh glad my youth.

dies away and is succeeded by a total lunar peace. The clouds scudding across a cold, luminous sky and the dark, uninhabited earth underneath are intended as a kind of snapshot of this planet after humanity has become extinct.

Years later, I discovered an interesting parallel to this "visionary" apprehension in one of the fantasies written down by Dr. Gerhard Adler's woman patient in *The Living Symbol.**

The narrator imagines herself, with companions, inside an immense sort of natural cathedral. They are told that a service will begin, and then, "It was as if a great invisible congregation was singing." Later, "the music died away" — and finally the whole cathedral dissolved, so that "There was nothing left but a clear sky with the sun shining in it; below was the earth, shining in the morning light as if it was the first day of creation."

Actually (as the full text shows) there was very much more to her experience than this: I have merely picked out the bare points of comparison with my own product. But the interesting thing is that, in his commentary on the "great invisible congregation," Dr. Adler describes this as "the expression of the experience that only in relationship to a community can the individual fulfill himself. The individual self cannot be realised in isolation but only as an integral individual part of mankind. Only as part of the *corpus mysticum*† in which every individual participates can it find its proper place and function, and, perhaps most important, every individual *does* have his place in the whole."

I don't think Dr. Adler's patient knew a great deal about the theological doctrine of the mystical body. She was not in the Catholic tradition, and I imagine it came as a surprise to her to find that her vision had a theological correlate. But the doctrine certainly meant something to me. One of the books that had most influenced me at Oxford was Karl Adam's *Spirit of Catholicism;* and one of the things it left in my mind was precisely a vivid concept of the unity of redeemed humanity in the mystical body of Christ.

---

*Routledge and Kegan Paul, London, 1961.
†Mystical body

The two fantasies both present the vision of a "great multitude whom no man can number." My Epilogue expressly identifies this with the whole human race; the other fantasy talks about a natural cathedral—i.e., the whole process is somehow organic. In each case, the music fades away and the vision is superseded. And in each case, the final scene shows the sky and the earth, void and untenanted.

Dr. Adler's patient was far advanced along a complicated pilgrimage of integration, the very existence of which was beyond my horizon at that time. But as his commentary points out, the dissolution of the cathedral means that the imaginative formulations she's worked out, however marvellous,* were only stages along the way, never something ultimate you could cling to.

The same line of argument applies to my case. Catholicism had showered its blue and golden richness upon me; but the time had now come to say farewell and to move onwards to the next stage.

Nox et tenebrae et nubila is in fact the epilogue to my love-affair with the Catholic Church. But at the same time, it shells out one aspect of the kernel of permanent meaning that lay wrapped up at the heart of this infatuation. Most noticeably, there is no explicit mention of Mother, of Church, or of any equivalent symbol—though the maternal influence still expresses itself to some extent in the romantic tone and feeling of the passage.

What does come over at this point as the nuclear essence of Catholicism is a vision of the mystical unity of humanity, a conception really common to all Christian denominations but conveniently forgotten for four centuries by the Protestants. I was well aware of this aspect, and had written letters on Catholic social theory to the "Cherwell" at Oxford.

But the date of this Epilogue (about September, 1942) may also be significant. Dr. Adler's patient had her cathedral fantasy in October, 1941. Of course, there was no conscious connection between the two. Yet both arrived in the middle of the war, at a time

---

*See for example the circular mosaic pavement from the cathedral, which she painted [*op. cit.,* p.45]

when Britain was fighting for her life against a despotism which denied the unity of humanity; at a time, too, when powerful currents of thought were moving towards a reaffirmation of community.

There's an interesting contrast between the tail-ends of the two fantasies — clear sky and shining sun and earth in the one, "as if it was the first day of creation"; misty sky, faint stars and dark earth in the other, the epic of creation being past and concluded. No doubt, there is at least some reference here to the life situation of the respective dreamers. In the course of her analysis, Dr. Adler's patient (who, by the way, was forty-nine) had won her way through, out of great perplexity, to a deeply-satisfying personal faith. The radiant finale symbolises her happiness and the rebirth of her personality. In my case, analysis had so far shifted the foundations that I was obliged to move on from the religion I had made my own and venture out into unknown dimensions. The finale, with its darkness and its suggestion of movement, may perhaps reflect this stage of transition.

XI
Dr. Laudenheimer ⸻

My time at the factory played itself out. As it happened, the Appointments Register at the Ministry of Labour found me a job at the University Correspondence Office at Cambridge. I made a lasting friend at the U.C.C. in the person of the war-time Scientific Director, Mr. D. Frenchman, a Parsee by extraction, but an adherent of our Western Enlightenment by conviction. He it was who recommended me to consult Dr. Rudolf Laudenheimer, an émigré psychotherapist who was living in Cambridge. I still badly wanted treatment, so I took my new friend's advice.

I am not likely to forget the first time I set eyes on Dr. Laudenheimer. He was walking along the street with his wife, and they had just reached the front gate of their house, which was in a second-class residential district. The impression I had was overwhelming — an elderly, devoted, bourgeois pair — so *Süddeutsch* — it was indescribable!

Could this oldish, conventional-looking man, with his sober, provincial clothes, possibly have the up-to-date knowledge and mastery of psychology to deal with the problems of modern people? I couldn't help feeling a little pang of disappointment.

All the same, I went on and introduced myself to him — I had very little alternative, really, since as far as I was aware there was no other psychotherapist at that time still practising in Cambridge. In fact, my relationship with Dr. Laudenheimer turned out to be, for good or ill, one of the most decisive in my life.

By school, he was a moderate follower of Jung. An excellent testimonial from Jung himself had helped him to get permission to practise psychotherapy in England (he was too old to retake his medical degree).

He was Jewish (his wife was not); but his whole culture and outlook were German, in the best sense of the word. He had stayed on in his sanatorium at Alsbach, near Munich, till January, 1939, after Jewish physicians had been forbidden to practise. Till then, he had been unable to believe that such a thing could happen in Germany. He had come to England with his wife, settled in Putney, built up a new practice, been bombed out, and had then been evacuated to Cambridge where, at the age of seventy or so, he had reestablished his life for the second time.

He was one of the finest human beings I have ever met — a cultivated liberal of the old German school. The two great passions of his life were psychology and literature. I always thought he might have stepped directly out of Goethe's circle at Weimar.

In actual treatment, I had a good deal of resistance against him. I was scarcely conscious of the fact that he was a Jungian; all the same, I did miss the familiar atmosphere of the old, well-tried Freudian approach, so that I couldn't give him my whole confidence. The truth is, I had come out of my Freudian analysis with certain very definite ideas on the How and the Why and the Should of the psyche. I was not particularly open to new suggestions.

I really haven't a very clear picture of the theories and techniques used by Dr. Laudenheimer. I know he wanted me to draw

something with real love. There he was unlucky—I wasn't ready
for it: the love just wasn't available. My resistance was so strong
at one point that I think Dr. Laudenheimer experimented with
treating me as "a Freudian case."

Another time, I remember him telling me that there was such
a thing as a Father archetype. My Freudian hackles were bristling
in a moment. I'd never read a reasoned exposition of what Jung
actually meant by his theory of archetypes, but that didn't prevent me at all from being intensely suspicious of the idea. Some
sort of mystical inherited ideas were being dragged into the discussion, I felt.

Altogether, I absorbed very few distinctively Jungian ideas. I
remember being told that as the treatment succeeded I should become rather more extraverted. I also heard something about the
"persona" (the mask, or social self, worn in front of the world).
In this connection, I did get one glimpse of Jung himself.

One of my troubles was bound up with a certain jacket which
I used to call my "gentleman coat," the point being that when
I wore it I felt stiff and uncomfortable in my relations with peo-
ple belonging to other social classes.

To illustrate flexibility in taking off and putting on a persona,
Dr. Laudenheimer told me a story about Jung arriving at a great
international congress of psychiatry, clad in a simple Swiss
peasant's cloak. Then, when he stepped up onto the platform,
he took off the cloak—and behold! he stood arrayed in full academic canonicals.

Years before that, Dr. Laudenheimer had seen Freud. "He had
magnificent, dark, melancholy eyes," he told me, in his deep German voice; "one would have loved him—But" (with emphasis)
"he was a Pope!"

As a matter of fact, the treatment continued the central line
of development I'd started before. The Tavistock analysis had
brought me to the point when I was actually trying to make friends
with girls. Dr. Laudenheimer's own strong, affirmative influence
tended entirely in the same direction.

I was now almost twenty nine, and I'd reached the point when I had a really desperate feeling that if I didn't make contact shortly, I should be shut out from relations with women for ever. So I deliberately took three days out of my holiday to go and stay with a Bohemian friend in Bayswater. My two ambitions for this brief excursion — to swim in the Serpentine and to meet a woman — were both (surprisingly) satisfied. I had an enjoyable dip in my friend's red and blue costume, which I draped at least one and a half times round my person; and, in his company, I also made a new woman friend.

This relationship later brought me the chance of having a full sexual experience. But I proposed to turn the opportunity down, as I didn't like the idea of using a contraceptive. I told Dr. Laudenheimer about this decision. For the one and only time in my life I saw him getting really angry.

"A nice wife [German *Weib* — a woman] will sleep with you, and you will not do it!" he exclaimed. "No wonder she does not like it! I think this is an excuse for avoiding an experience which you fear."

This put a new complexion on the matter, with a vengeance! It was a complete reversal of the authority situation as I had always known it. My father-figure had actually pronounced in favour of sexual intercourse! And at the same time, he had cast aspersions on my courage. The combination of these two potent factors was irresistible. I reversed my previous decision. "If that's what you think, I'll jolly well show you!" — this, spoken or tacit, approximately expressed my attitude.

Shortly afterwards, I had the experience which must be crucial to any man, let alone one with my history. It was not without its richly comic, and also its tragic aspects; and it certainly didn't clear up my problems. But there's no doubt, it was the birth of a new stage of development for me. This came out very clearly in a dream I had about this time. I was nearly late for the factory (so I dreamed), but a big single-bar gate swung back to let through, and I was admitted to a lovely, fresh, emerald-green, dewy, sparkling lawn on the left.

The affair came to a rather sorrowful end not very long afterwards. But the change in principle (from my point of view) was immense. I was now, in the time-honoured phraseology of the Unemployment Assistance Board, "capable of, and available for" a full (though not necessarily adult) sexual relationship.

I became a personal friend of Dr. and Mrs. Laudenheimer's, and often had tea at their house. They had no children of their own, and I was really like a adopted son. What a wonderful experience it was to partake of the warmhearted, vital *Gemütlichkeit* of that family!* It was a mystery how, in the midst of war and rationing, Mrs. Laudenheimer and her faithful Bavarian maid managed to furnish out that tea-table, with its piled-up riches of buns and cakes. It was also a mystery to the established British long-resident neighbours how this old refugee couple, starting a new life at well over retirement age, still contrived to have a house full of young people.

I remember Mrs. Laudenheimer — a splendid woman, with the courage of a lion — teaching me Goethe when I left at the conclusion of my analytic hour:

> Alles geben die Götter, die unendlichen
> Ihren lieblingen *ganz;*
> Alle freuden, die unendlichen,
> Alle Schmerzen, die unendlichen, *ganz.*
> (All things the gods, the immortals,
> Give to their darlings, to the uttermost;
> All joys, the immortals,
> All sorrows, the immortals,
> To the uttermost.)

The ridiculous bathos of "to the uttermost" only underlines the colossal punch of the German monosyllable *ganz,* coming like a

---

*This untranslatable German word denotes a kind of rosy good-humour, an easy, companionable acceptance both of people and of the good things of life. You could say it is the opposite of the Prussian virtues!

knock-out blow to settle the hash of each half of this bipartite sentence. The word, with that immense pile-driver emphasis ramming it home every time, is itself a kind of symbol of totality.

"I am a King!" Mrs. Laudenheimer told me, "You are a King! Everybody is a King!—You look the world in the face!" What splendid advice that was to give that poor, shrinking young man!

It really did seem at that time as if the past had begun to release its tentacles. After a bit more than a year at Cambridge, I felt better and more positive, somehow, and I conceived the notion of applying to the military authorities and asking for a second military examination. I didn't any longer see any reason why I should stand aside from the destiny which other men of my generation were facing.

Dr. Laudenheimer was extremely pleased; he said it meant I was getting out of the safety-first mentality he had noticed in me. It's a curious fact that having now had intercourse with a woman, I was, to that extent, satisfied, and no longer required to reproach the Mother-country with having deprived me of the rights of man!

I was duly reexamined and up-graded from Grade IV to Grade II; the doctor on the medical board congratulated me on my spirit. Six weeks later, I was called up into the Army.

XII
The Army _____

I 've sometimes wondered at what precise point I ceased to "have a neurosis," as distinct from being a rather nervous person, with some neurotic traits and symptoms.

I think perhaps my volunteering for reexamination is a good, pragmatic dividing-line. It was the most decisive act in my life, up till then. It meant abandoning all cover and coming right out into the open. I did it without any afterthoughts or secret escape-clauses. If it's possible, by a single act of will, to opt to be a grown-up man, then this was it — and I'd done it!

I can say that I persisted doggedly with my German; this provided the link with the inner world which I must have if I am to survive. I used to read my little books at break-times in the canteen, and I had them in the barrack-room with me. Our Sergeant did not approve — he associated everything German with the Nazis.

In one vital respect, at any rate, the British Army had moved with the times: it had entered into a *mariage de convenance* with psychology. Surely two more oddly-assorted spouses can never have hopped into bed with one another! Yet, as sometimes happens, the results were excellent.

My medical record was available to the authorities; now, like all the other recruits, I was put through the whole battery of the Army's Personnel Selection tests. These tests are very efficient, and sort people out in a most practical way. In World War I, I could have been drafted to the trenches, where I might easily have started a panic and got shot — probably by the British. This time, without any fuss or false heroics, I was quietly assigned to clerical duties.

I now found myself landed as a private in the Pay Corps. My heroism had recoiled upon me full circle. I had volunteered to get away from office routine and out into the life of adventure, and behold, a great monstrous schoolmarm called Psychological Selection, with an arm like a steel excavator, had picked me up by the scruff of the neck and dumped me down in an office again!

I stuck it for about eleven months. In the meantime, I was still just as keen as ever on learning German, and it was this that turned out to be the dynamic thread that was to lead me forwards into the future. I was extremely excited by the opportunity that came along to see my first German film — it was Fritz Kortner in Dostoevsky's "Die Brüder Karamasow." Tickets for the film were to be obtained at the "Freier Deutscher Kulturbund" (the Free German League of Culture, a wartime refugee organisation at Belsize Park). I went along to collect mine. A woman who by chance happened to be doing duty in the library handed me the tickets. She asked my advice on books to read in English. I recommended Evelyn Waugh's *Decline and Fall,* and *Vile Bodies.* We went on talking, and became friends. Five months later, we were married.

My wife was born in Berlin. In a sense, you can say that we are both refugees. But having by a strange fatality found each other, we set up house together in a modest way, and in so doing discovered something else. If you've got a home, there's at any rate one spot on earth where you aren't a refugee any longer.

One immediate result of my marriage was that I learned many more German words — including slang and domestic expressions. I became more and more dissatisfied with my clerk's office, and I longed to put my knowledge to effect in the war. I had the idea of becoming an interpreter; from the Pay Corps point of view, however, I was (or at least was said to be!) far too valuable as a Grade II clerk.

Somehow I got an interview with an Army psychiatrist, a Roman Catholic as a matter of fact. I can truthfully say that he was one of the most brilliant specimens I have ever encountered in all my experience of the psychiatric fraternity.

He asked me what conflicts I was suffering from, and when I couldn't think of any, he promptly clamped down and said I had none, but that the motive spring of all my actions was a deep-seated feeling of guilt. He was kind enough to temper this slightly intimidating *pronunciamento* by conceding that this ultimate whatever-it-was was not necessarily incompatible with creative work.

When it came to the interpretership, the psychiatrist tried to rally me out of the idea. "Be your age!" he said. I couldn't get the bearings of that remark, quite.

I think now he suspected guilt was driving me into unrealistic heroics. Yet really, in undertaking both these adventures I had acted progressively — along the line, that is, which offered me a possibility of positive development. At the time, I was so sure I was right that I couldn't see what he was getting at. I could only insist that I really did want to become an interpreter. We carried on talking, and had a little chat about Immanuel Kant and the problem of free will. I think both of us found this refreshing; it was certainly a welcome break from Army routine. The upshot of the interview was that he wrote me a certificate to the effect that I was unemployable in the Army in any other capacity than as an interpreter.

This put the Pay corps pundits on the spot. To do him justice, my Captain was very decent about it, and most willing to do the right thing. He explained that the only way he could get rid of me was by degrading me on the grounds of inefficiency; it would have to come out in Company Orders. I answered, "For the Lord's sake, sir, degrade me as soon as you possibly can!" (or words to that effect.)

I was given a brief language test in German at Hobart House (where the National Coal Board is now, opposite the back garden wall of Buckingham Palace). I didn't have to write a single word; the questions were simply designed to weed out those whose knowledge of the language did not exceed the level of "*Ich liebe Dick.*" At one point I failed: I couldn't provide the German equivalent of "I ought to have done it." The examiner told me it was "*Ich hätte es tun sollen.*" He also told me I had passed the test.

So the deed was done, and I was duly degraded. The Captain gave me his personal promise that if anything went wrong with my posting as an interpreter, he would reinstate me in the Pay Corps in my original rank.

XIII
A Book by Jung _____

T he combination of German and analysis brought me
straight into the middle of "reality" and "life." But it
had also brought me right up against the problem of
a deep human relationship with a person of the opposite sex — and around this problem. All my remaining psychological difficulties were clustered like barnacles on the keel of a sunken
vessel.

In plain language, I fell into a deep depression. But if you take
the literal meaning of this last word (depression — a sunken declivi-
ty), you arrive back quite close to my figurative expression. I was
scuppered; and as Sargant has pointed out in his suggestive study
of brainwashing down the ages;* depression is very often a precon-
dition of conversion.

The year was 1946; I was on leave, and at the moment when

_____
*The Battle for the Mind, by J.S. Sargant, Heinemann, London 1957; Pan Books, Lon-
don 1959.

I was just about touching my nadir, a book belonging to an English woman friend of my wife's just happened to come into my hands. The book was called *The Integration of the Personality;* and its author was Carl G. Jung.

I can safely say that nothing I've ever read either before or since can compare with the total, knock-out impact Jung's book made on me at that moment. For better or for worse, it bowled me right over, and let to a climacteric change in my whole orientation.

In itself, *The Integration of the Personality* is one of the most brilliant productions in Jung's long and fertile career. The title is significant. The book actually consists of a series of papers centring round the theme of individuation — the process by which a human being crystallises out into a unique Self.

Of course, my mind had been prepared for Jung by Freud's schematic map or diagram of the psyche. In practice, what I saw, or rather felt, was nothing particularly sharp or graphic. But for clarity's sake, it can be represented as a circle, the top third of which was left blank, or white, and stood for the realm of the conscious mind, while the bottom two thirds were dark or shaded, and symbolised "the unconscious." Two dots or small circles in the upper portion signified — in ascending order — the ego and the superego, and deep down in the shady part, another nodule represented the "id," or "old Uncle Libido."

When I read Jung's book, it was as if Jung himself stepped up to the blackboard on which I had inscribed my diagram, took a look at it, said "Excellent! — except that your circle has no centre," and then chalked in a small golden "x," exactly at the mathematical middle of the diagram. "This," he went on to explain, as it were, "is a centre of the total personality which is other than the ego, and which in fact embraces both the conscious and the unconscious mind. In the language of religion it is known as God."

The image of Jung correcting my diagram bears the same kind of relation to the actual event as I imagine is borne by the physicist's model of waves and particles to the real mini-happenings he is trying to describe. It is a concession to the weakness of our conceiving apparatus, which can only think of reality in terms of illusion.

Never before and never since has any interpretation or experience in my life "clicked" with the unconscious as this one did. "God" had been reinterpreted in a meaningful way, in terms of the total personality of man. It was as if the two great vital obsessions of my life—psychology and Christianity—had unexpectedly united their forces, like two rivers rushing joyfully into each other's arms. And the point of confluence was C.G. Jung.

Part Two:

Reinterpretation

XIV
After-effects of Illumination _____

A
fter I read *The Integration of the Personality,* my whole life changed its direction. I don't mean I gave all my goods to the poor, or that I went about doing good. I mean that such a great light had dawned upon me that I felt as if I had solved the religious problem and bridged the gulf between faith and unbelief.

In the whole of my life, I have never felt such supreme confidence about anything. Suddenly, all sorts of things seemed to be clear, and I was gifted with the power of interpretation — a power and a gift which had certainly never visited me to this extent before. Of course, the interpretations may have been wrong. In fact, if at the age of thirty two you imagine you've solved the riddle of the universe, this very finality is a proof of incompleteness: by going too far, you supply convincing evidence that in fact you've not gone far enough.

If you think of it in terms of the old-fashioned gaslight, then

Jung's book was the match applied to the mantle. But the incandescent, white-hot flame which sprang up instantaneously and illuminated the mantle so brilliantly from inside was a process touched off inside my own psyche.

XV
The Reinterpretation
of Christianity _____

"The Idea of Humanity" _____

fter three years' service I was demobilised from the
Army. I had applied for (and obtained) a job as a Training Adviser (for the reeducation of German prisoners
of war) in the Political Intelligence Department of the
Foreign Office.

My demobilisation leave was in front of me (May and June,
1947). I realised that I might never again in my life have as much
as eight solid uninterrupted weeks continuously at my disposal.
So I decided to use the time to write a book—a psychological
reinterpretation of Christianity, no less! The title was (originally) *The Idea of Humanity.*

The stuff seemed to squirt straight out like liquid toothpaste
squeezed from a tube. It was far more spontaneous and immediate than anything I've written before or since. But it was not just
a formless romantic flux. There was some kind of thought and
structure behind it. I was able now to make use of some insights

71

I'd picked up from Christopher Dawson's teaching (in *Progress and Religion* and *The Making of Europe*) about the function of religion as the spiritual dynamic of society. In particular I could point to the Catholic faith as the creative force which had shaped the supranational unity of Europe; yet I was no longer tempted to advocate any purely reactionary return to the past. I was able to explain how the great Christian and Catholic projections had been stripped away successively, like the layers of an onion, till the point was reached when nothing was left and we were confronted with a consuming void. In proportion that we turned our backs on God, God's backside was turned on us.

The credit for this liberation into writing belongs fairly and squarely to Jung's book. Analysis had loosened my mother-fixation to the point where writing about the subjects I cared for was no longer intrinsically psychological incest. But it was Jung who put into my hands the unifying principle which enabled me to sort things out and make some kind of order out of myself and my experience.

It's significant that I wanted to share my discovery with other people. I think to some extent this feeling is justified. My experience was not just a matter of my personal psychology; it linked up with the religious problem of many other modern people.

It seems to me that the concept of God is rejected nowadays for two main reasons. This concept — at any rate as traditionally projected by theology — does seem to most people to run clean counter to both reality and life.

The "real" world that we look out on with our ordinary eyes and walk about in one our everyday feet just doesn't seem to square up with the idea of a Christian God. Put it this way. Let us suppose that we're all religious innocents, with our eyes clear and naive and unclouded (either way) by the vested interests of the traditional past. Now would anybody, honestly, on the normal evidence of his senses, contrive to hit upon the notion that this world is best explained as the creation of an infinitely loving, perfect Heavenly Father? As I said in *The Idea of Humanity*, nature gives the impression of being grown rather than made. And the sufferings of animals and of millions of tiny insects (which present no kind of difficulty on a naturalistic hypothesis) are completely incompatible with infinite love.

It is perhaps the supreme negative achievement of Christianity that it has managed to present God as relentlessly hostile to *both* the two fundamental surges of life, ego and sex. This turns God into a kind of celestial head-master, the apotheosis of the super-ego and the censor and the sum total of all the repressive forces. To this extent — and it's a large one — Freud's identification of God with the father-complex is justified. But we have to remember that God is not necessarily confined to any one idea or culture. And in my own case, although both the Father and the Mother had obviously played an enormous part in my psychology, it had never occurred to me to identify God with either of these images, complexes, archetypes or what have you. Yet after reading Jung's book, I did feel, with terrific force, that God corresponded to what he said about the centre of the total personality.

Now this new interpretation seems to throw a flood of light on the religious problem I've been outlining. In fact, it disposes of the opposition between religion and reality and life in one and the same fell swoop. And it does this without undermining the essential validity of religious experience — where it is valid. It does (to some extent) explain: it does *not* explain away.

If, as I tried to show, goodness is an internal human category, then the problem of evil disappears. And if God is associated with a natural, quasi-organic centring process — like growth on a metabiological level — then the split between religion and life can also be shown to derive from a mistake. God (in this hypothesis) is in the deepest sense not to be identified with the patriarchal forbidding authority, but with the psyche as a potential whole. This conception would demolish once and for all the old-fashioned religious bias against ego and sex. In any moral conflict, the final court of appeal will be, not the traditional value-judgements of society, but the agent's own true, ultimate self.

But the argument from life cuts both ways. It isn't merely that the traditional distortion of Christianity had split religion off from life. Life, by the same token, had been split off from religion. So I tried to show that when, for instance, reason and will are divorced from their matrix in the total psyche, an unbalanced and inflated idolatry of the conscious mind is likely to result. Each little ego is then pent up in a kind of scorched white concrete pill-box, which it identifies with the universe. So a religion which is out of touch with life is confronted by a vitality which has lost contact with meaning. But if you think of God as the centre of our personality, then you have the vital focus needed, where religion inevitably touches life, and life must encounter the meaning of things.

XVI
Wilton Park _____

A Gospel for the Germans _____

My leave came to an end at last, and with it, my inspiration. It wasn't that I'd lost faith in the book, but that the flow simply dried up, so that what I wrote subsequently was different in character. And anyway, life took up the batting now, and I went off to my duties as a Training Adviser in various POW camps. I did this highly-paid work for six months, but I certainly wasn't an outstanding success.

Yet the job did lead on to something more fruitful. This was an appointment as Tutor at Wilton Park, a camp near Beaconsfield which was the seat of the famous Foreign Office School of Democracy for German Prisoners, or *Demokratenschule*, as the Germans liked to call it.

In effect, this was a kind of university of reeducation in a highly potted form. Prisoners selected for their intelligence and cooperativeness were given six-week courses of lectures and discussions centring broadly on the democratic way of life.

To a large extent, the seven or eight Tutors were given a free hand to develop their subjects as they pleased. One was a Tory, one a Social Democrat, one a Quaker, and so on. People of the calibre of Victor Gollancz and Canon Raven were invited down to speak at Wilton Park, or to take part in brains trusts.

As a Tutor, I had to take my own class in a current affairs discussion, and I also lectured, to other groups, on *Internationale Bürgerkunde* (International Civics). All this side of the work was conducted in German.

But my own individual contribution came out in my first lecture, which was largely devoted to a *Philosophische Einführung in die Politik* (Philosophical Introduction to Politics). Such a title may sound pompous in English. But with the Germans, things were rather different. In the first place, any German with any pretensions to education and intelligence was expected to have a *Weltanschauung*. And in the second place, all these *Weltanschauungen* had been cracked to the foundations by the triumph and destruction of Nazi Germany.

I was trying to demolish some of the basic postulates of totalitarianism, and at the same time to replace them by something positive.

I began by pointing out that authoritarian leaders and authoritarian parties were substitute fathers and mothers for grown-up children. I went on: *"Es ist aber die verdammte pflicht eines erwachsenen Mannes, selbst zu denken, selbst zu fühlen, und selbst zu handeln" ("But it's damn well the duty of a grown-up man to think for himself, to feel for himself, and to act for himself")*.

I then launched out into my *Philosophische Einführung in die Politik,* which I divided into two sections: biology and psychology.

Under biology, I argued that though in ants the organism is the anthill, in human beings the organism is the family.*

---

*The identification of the organism in man with the family was a doctrine taught by the founders of the Pioneer Health Centre, at Peckham.

The family, together with its psychological derivative, the group (by which I meant a smallish association, made up of some five to twenty persons), provides the natural community setting within which human qualities can fully ripen. The State, on the other hand, is not an organic social unit at all, but a congeries of individual persona, families and groups. The State must therefore conform to the nature of its constituents, and not vice versa.

Under psychology, I made some use of the tool which Jung had put into my hands. I pointed out that primitive man has no concept for the unconscious. He therefore (I contended) projects this unconscious outwards in the form of God. Modern man rejects God, but needs a god (*i.e.*, a concept for his total personality) just as much as primitive man does. Into the psychological vacuum which is thus created, there slips the devilish temptation to raise the State to the power of God. This makes "my country" into a religion — *i.e.*, a cause which demands man's total allegiance. Once this has happened, the State can perfectly well require the commission of the most frightful atrocities — such as the extermination of entire races or classes — and there is no means of redress left.

The moral is clear. I argued for the absolute necessity of a true religion; and I went on boldly to define true religion as: "In all circumstances to be true to one's own soul." I backed up this conclusion with two quotations — first, the well-known lines from Hamlet:

> To thine own self be true,
> And it shall follow, as the night the day,
> Thou canst not then be false to any man

and second, a hexameter from the Bavarian poetess Ricarda Huch:

> Niemals treulos und feige den Gott in der Brust zu verleugnen.
> (Never, like a traitor or a coward, deny the God in your breast).

The only reaction I can remember from my audience was a criticism one student made to the effect that Jung said "*das Dämonische*" (the daemonic) was to be found in the unconscious as well as was the divine. This, of course, is perfectly true; but the criticism caught me unawares, and I reacted rather huffily, with something like a denial. My mind was so entirely taken up with reinterpreting "God," as he had come to me in my own (Christian) experience that I simply didn't think about other aspects. It didn't enter my mind that even Christian theology has a place for the Devil! My critic had touched me on a blind spot—if that's not too mixed-up a metaphor.

XVII
Civvy Street _____

I was sorry in a way when, with the winding-up of repatriation, my appointment at Wilton Park was terminated. I'd been there for just under six months, from January to June, 1948. But the fact of the matter is that my deeper interests were no longer with the German question.

While I was still at my second camp (which was at Crookham Common, in Berkshire), I'd had a short and pithy dream, in which I'd explained to an American, "Yes! but there's not only engineering—there's also psychiatry!" At the time it definitely impressed me as containing vocational guidance for myself. I took the message quite literally: I, Eugene Rolfe, was to become a psychiatrist!

I secured interviews with representatives of the Institute of Psychoanalysis; the Society of Analytical Psychology; the Tavistock Clinic; the Oxford Institute of Experimental Psychology; and the Maudsley Hospital.

I'd covered quite a lot of ground; but the result was a foregone conclusion. I lacked the money for a training analysis. I was still, incidentally, far too neurotic to be anywhere near the starting-line for this profession, of all things.

I knew this perfectly well, of course; or at least, the knowledge was inside me somewhere. The surprising thing is that it didn't inhibit me at the outset from plunging into this crackpot scheme. My genuine (though misdirected) sense of vocation must have been strong enough to carry me along regardless. In my more cynical moments, I must confess, I do still sometimes wonder whether neuroticism by itself would have been such an insuperable obstacle, provided the money had been forthcoming.

I now found myself in the fatal situation of the arts graduate who is inhibited from the professional exercise of his Art, and discovers that he is qualified for nothing. After a couple of months as a temporary male clerk at the Admiralty (where, incidentally, I was treated exceedingly well), I landed a job teaching Latin at a high-class preparatory establishment attached to a large London public school.

When the time came for me to take up my duties, I was brought up against a complete immovable psychological block—like a wall of granite barring my path. Expressed in words, this categorical imperative in the negative might have run, "Thou shalt not teach Latin!" Once more my erring footsteps had struck up against the implacable adamantine rock-barrier of the psychological incest taboo. It was humiliating for me, and awkward for the headmaster of the school, who had passed over two other candidates in my favour, but I was simply compelled to ring up and call off the whole appointment. I was sorry, but I really had no alternative.

By this time, I'd read some of Jung's other books. There was a nice little nest of them, I discovered, in the Chester Road Branch of the St. Pancras Public Library. One passage, I remember, which came home to me personally, was where Jung categorically stated that no-one who had a tendency towards mental trouble should be allowed to absent himself from his *regular work* for a single day on that account.

A few months later, for reasons of security, I took and passed one of the post-war reconstruction examinations for temporary civil servants, and was established in the clerical officer grade, one step above the bottom rung on which I had entered. I was precluded by age from taking further examinations.

In the most extraordinary way, it was as if the whole process of my education, right up to and including university honours standard, had been boiled down to its lowest possible denominator—the simple ability to guide a pen.

This situation did, to some extent, put me on my mettle. I felt I'd had to put up some kind of a struggle to bring my university qualification to bear upon my working life. But this degree, which had come to be so important to me, was in reality a certificate of proficiency. *"Do vobis potestatem,"* the Vice-Chancellor had said, *"legendi, disputandi, et omnia faciendi, quae in facultate artium requiruntur, in nomine Patris, et Filii, et Spiritus Sancti."* ("I grant you the power to read, to dispute and to do all things which are requisite in the Faculty of Arts, in the name of the Father, and of the Son, and of the Holy Ghost.") As he mentioned each separate person of the Trinity, the Vice-Chancellor had brought his prayer-book down on the head of one of the candidates kneeling in front of him; the book came down on my head at the name of the Father, I remember. I'd always taken this in exactly the sense which it must have had originally, in the Middle Ages—*i.e.,* as a kind of priestly investiture, or initiation into the mysteries of learning. It was essentially a *licence to perform;* and I never doubted for a moment that, given a suitable opportunity, I could indeed provide a performance. So the vital issue, you could say, was ultimately reducible to a question of *potency.* Could I connect my firepower with the target?

In 1949, the year I joined the Ministry of Labour, I started to grow a beard. The onset of the affair was unadulterated laziness. I was down at Bognor Regis, and I said to myself, "I'm on holiday. Why should I bother to shave?" But I continued to grow this beard when I got back to London; and that, of course, was a more serious matter. It meant that I didn't see myself as a typical civil servant, and that I didn't want to be mistaken for one, either. I think that, behind this underlining of difference, there was an implied assertion of potentiality in some other, not clearly specified, direction.

During my first two or three years at the Ministry, I applied for quite a number of appointments — art gallery assistant, commissioned teacher in the Army, civil service information officer, etc. As time went by and I found I was not merely being passed over, but that I was regularly being denied even the recognition of an interview, I began to get discouraged. It wasn't until a year or two later that I happened to meet an old acquaintance of mine — a man out of my year at Keble, as it happened — who opened my eyes to the simple fact that a salary ceiling must have been operating against me. By accepting a lower grade of employment, or rather, a lower rate of remuneration, I had virtually excluded myself from the field.

For years, I felt frightfully sore and aggrieved about this. After all, I'd been advised to take up this type of work to fill in time before my next appointment. And now the beastly job had destroyed my chances! I was carrying around somewhere inside myself a loathsome, damp, smouldering fuse of resentment and disappointment. Yet if I look back, it seems obvious to me that I was straining after the empty shell of status, and disregarding the one thing needful — the essential, nutrient kernel of vocation.

At one point, it is true, I did get a little closer to the mark. I enrolled for a post-graduate diploma in psychology at Birkbeck College, London University. I was inspired by the laudable ambition of learning psychology from top to bottom with professional thoroughness, as Jung had done. If I'd been younger, and could have studied full-time, I might perhaps have brought this off. But I, unfortunately, was neither Jung or young!

In his early period, Jung had got through an enormous volume of painstaking, detailed, meticulous work in connection with his association experiments.* Experimental work was entirely new to me. The unfamiliar labour of constructing diagrams and recording results in notebooks, etc., would have driven me completely crazy. I certainly learned something from the lectures I attended; at least I discovered the existence of experimental psychology. But the experiment of attempting to climb into psychiatry by means of the ladder of psychological engineering had to be added to the catalogue of my extraverted failures.

When I'd been in the Ministry about three years, I wrote a memorandum to the authorities drawing attention to my language qualifications. As a result, I was offered (and accepted) the post of Overseas Librarian in the Ministry's Overseas Department. After some time I was given German translations to do. After some more time, I took over all the routine work of translating references, etc., from German, French and Italian. I was rewarded by a language allowance, and also by a sprinkled-in seasoning of other-than-routine translations, at intervals. In a small way, I'd succeeded in achieving a special position — which is the only workable alternative to guerrilla warfare between an academic deviationist such as myself and the orthodox civil service. I'd gained a small but invaluable toe-hold inside my own sacred territory, and from this point of vantage I was able to apply and extend my knowledge of languages in an elementary but serviceable fashion. To me, the work was interesting and satisfying; and its social utility could not be denied. I'd found my level in the extraverted world — and a pretty humble one it was at that.

---

*The results are recorded in "Experimental Researches," CW II, Routledge and Kegan Paul, London, 1973

XVIII
A Letter from Zurich _____

I 've skipped ahead for a year or two, up to the stage when I'm finally settled in my modest niche in the post-war world. But I need hardly say that the strange interior psychological pilgrimage which had preoccupied me for so long had not a simply evaporated in the interval.

I continued writing *The Idea of Humanity;* I was hard at work at it at Wilton Park that June, 1948, after the prisoners had left. I finished it that summer. The last part of the book was far more a matter of constructional argument, a kind of moral blue-print for the post-war world.

I'd discovered the reality of the God within and applied this to the First Christian Commandment (Thou shalt love the Lord thy God with all thy heart and with all thy mind and with all thy soul and with all thy strength). I now went on to try to prove from this reinterpreted First Commandment the validity of the Second Christian Commandment (Thou shalt love thy neighbour as thyself). Finally, I proceeded to attempt to justify the whole Christian doctrine of the family, in detail. This meant I had to argue pro monogamy, fidelity and premarital chastity and contra masturbation, adultery, homosexuality, lesbianism, etc. etc.

I posted the completed manuscript to Victor Gollancz (the choice was obvious, since I had a slight but recent acquaintance with V.G.). Nothing happened for what seemed to be to be ages; then after some prodding, the manuscript was returned, with an extract from the report of Gollancz's reader (a theologian, I imagine). Put briefly, the verdict ran something like this: "Good in parts, but, as an account of God, scarcely adequate."

I was practically in despair. So much had depended on the answer; and the answer had been negative! My masterpiece had been rejected! It was a crushing blow to all my hopes. I didn't know what on earth I should do with the manuscript; it didn't occur to me to send it to another publisher. But then I had a sudden flash of inspiration; I bundled it up and sent it off to Jung himself, in Zürich. He, if anyone, would be able to appreciate what I'd written.

I wrote Jung a letter in my not altogether flawless German. I explained how the book had arisen out of my life, and I told him one or two dreams. In particular, there was one remarkable one I'd had during my Wilton Park period.

After an initial episode dealing with personal matters, the dream-scene had shifted to a kind of cabin-place, underground. Here a wordy conflict was in progress between two upstanding antagonists. On the left was the slim outline of a white masculine god — only shadowily sketched in, with the bottom part not indicated at all. It seemed like a kind of father-figure. On the right, over against him, was a brown fulminating female demon, positively writhing and vibrating with energy and power. Whereas the father-god was like a form emptied of content, the demonic mother had far more substance and life than would be met with in any "real" figure.

The two were hurling insults at each other, but without action.

They didn't touch each other, and not a blow was struck on either side. Yet the violence of the conflict was so severe that the whole cabin rocked convulsively from side to side. It reminded me in a way of a Punch and Judy show—though there was absolutely nothing comic about it.

The outcome of the struggle was completely unexpected. The white god succeeded in silencing the brown demon. And then a most curious development occurred. Like a kind of emanation from the brown side, a slender snake arose, of the same dark substance as the demon, transferring itself to the white side in the direction of the outline father. The snake's head had the face of a young Jewish man of my acquaintance (a member of the staff at Wilton Park), who was very much on the democratic side in the struggle between the Western Powers and Communism.

Naturally enough, this dream made a great impression on me. It is the only dream I can remember which forced me involuntarily to think of Jung's archetypes. There was something (a kind of mythological quality) about the figures, and also about the intensity of the conflict which simply *was* archetypal.

So I bundled up the manuscript (letter and all) and registered it, using string in four colours, red, blue, yellow and green (all rather faint)—the four colours of totality, according to Jung. The parcel looked faintly auspicious, I thought.

I didn't have very long to wait. A letter, dated October 25th, 1948, came back from Jung's secretary at Küsnacht, Zürich. It said:

Dear Sir,
   Professor Jung asked me to let you know that your manuscript has safely reached him and that he has been very much interested by what you write to him. Although his time does not permit him to read manuscript he will try to make an exception in your case and hopes to be able to write to you personally without undue delay.
                    Yours sincerely,
                    M-j. Schmidt,
                    Secretary

I was overjoyed by this letter. Jung himself was interested in what I had written! That was sweet, sweet, sweet. But my mind was so obsessively concentrated on my *book* that I referred everything to that masterpiece and disregarded the letter which I'd written to accompany it.

On the face of it, "What you write to him" must have related to the letter, not the book. I now just had to possess my soul in patience, a form of passivity in which I persisted for four months longer.

Finally, another letter arrived from Zürich. Like the first, it carried the blue, 40-centime Helvetia stamp that was so exciting and evocative, with its view of the lake and the towering mountains. It consisted of a full page, closely typed in English, and signed by the great man himself. It was on Jung's personal headed notepaper. It ran as follows:

Prof. Dr. C.G. Jung   Küsnacht-Zürich
                                                       Seestrasse 228
                                                       March 3rd, 1949

Mr. Eugene M.E. Rolfe,
19, Tremlett Grove,
London, N.19

Dear Mr. Rolfe,

I'm sorry to have kept your manuscript so long, but I wanted to have it thoroughly searched, in which purpose I have been helped by a friend.

The first part of your book is a quite interesting attempt to apply the idea of wholeness to the individual in the light of your own experience, but in the second part you fall more and more a victim to the idea of a collective solution.

You say in your letter that you had a dream while writing the first stages of your book, namely that you were going to have a baby, small but like yourself, and that at the end your were afraid that it was a miscarriage. I'm afraid that these dreams apply to your book inasmuch as the second part and the end are premature attempts to translate your individual experiences into a collective application, which is impossible. You cannot teach a certain kind of morality or belief, you must be it. If you are it, then you can say what you want and it works. But you are not out of the wood yet. For instance, you entirely neglect the fact that man has an anima that plays the dickens with him — for instance, you married her — and the shadow rolled into one. Under those conditions it is almost impossible to realize one's own anima, because her reality is all the time right under your nose and it is always pointed out to you that she is your wife.

It is a great temptation in our days, when on [sic] talks to Germans, to look for a sort of collective teaching or a collective ideal, but you find only words that don't carry. But if you are a really integrated personality, in other words, if you know all about your shadow and all about your anima (which is worse), then you have a hope to be the truth, namely truly yourself, and that is a thing that works. I could repeat the words of an early Christian Papyrus which says: "Therefore thrive [sic] thee first to know yourselves, because ye are the city and the city is the kingdom."

I should advise you to consult at once Dr. Gerhard Adler (29, Welbeck Street, London, W.1.), especially with reference to the problem of shadow and anima.

I hope you will mind the almost rude directness of my letter. It is well-meant, as I know that if you should succeed in publishing the book as it is now, it would be no success whatever, or it would have a wrong effect. I should therefore advise you to keep the manuscript unpublished until the most important question of the shadow and the anima has been duly settled.

Sincerely yours,
C.G. Jung.

The MS is being returned to you separately.

It's a tribute to the strength of my attachment for Dr. Jung that I was able to take this letter without experiencing grievous disappointment. Of course, I was enormously pleased at receiving such a long and detailed missive from the great man himself. And I was delighted at the excellent colloquial English in which it was written. And, of course, the letter wasn't negative in its impact. Jung had told me what was right about the book before explaining where it had left the track. And he had given me a perfectly definite, practical suggestion for action—something I could do about it.

I was able to accept the justice of Jung's criticism of my book without any difficulty. I had only to reflect to realise quite plainly that what I'd written after the big initial spurt had been, in fact, a conscious construction—a piece of intellectual carpentering, really, designed to underpin traditional Christianity with a naturalistic substructure, now that its metaphysical foundations were presumed to have fallen away.

The change of mood from Part One is signaled by the far more frequent use of normative auxiliaries—such as "should," "will," "must," "ought," etc.—in the later stages of the book. Part One sprang, flowed, emanated straight out of the heart of my own experience. In Part Two, I am legislating for other people, like a schoolmaster preaching a kind of morality he has not lived out himself—which is what Jung himself suggests.

The dream itself can be interpreted on a number of different levels. The outline god and the demoness can obviously be Father and Mother, and the wordy battle between them the actual conflict between the parents. There's truth in this, up to a point. The outline god does bear a slight resemblance to my personal father; my personal mother's vitality could certainly at times be described as demonic; and there had undoubtedly been a conflict between them.

On the other hand, in real life my father was anything but an impotent silhouette; and the female figure in the dream was entirely unlike my mother in appearance. We may be able to throw some light on this difficulty if we bring in another pair of alternative explanations—the inward and the outward interpretation of a dream. The outward sees the parental figures impinging on the child. The inward looks for the meaning of these figures in the structure of the child's own personality.

The first thing we notice, from this point of view, is the mythological aura of the figures. They are not personal photographs out of the family album, but archaic images evoked by my parents in my psyche as a child. An ideal father-god who lacks earthly substance is confronted by a raving female chthonic fiend who lacks positive human attributes. In terms of the present, these two antagonists obviously reflect the basic dichotomy between my respectable Western conscious outlook and the instinctual dynamism bottled up in the unconscious.

If you look at it historically, on the other hand, the quarreling couple do add up quite a neat reversal of what I remember about the primary Oedipus situation. Clearly, they originate from the post-Oedipal stage, when I'd nominally gone over to my father's camp, and was siding with him against my mother. To any male creature, masculinity must be important; he must develop it if he is to fulfill his biological and psychological functions. So my father, the representative of manhood to and in myself, appears in my young psyche in the shape of a god. But I was too soft, and too attached to my mother, to realise this malehood in action. Hence my father remains an empty, though ideal, scheme, a reflection of my immature masculine development. For maturity, or realisation, the god would have to become a man.

But the female is also frightfully important to the male. Without her, no new life can be born, on the biological or psychological levels. Yet in my dream, the female takes the form, not of a goddess, but of a demonic fiend. This means that to me, in the post-Oedipal phase, my mother's passionate instinctive vitality seemed to be destructive and subversive of what I thought of at the time as my father's altogether reasonable and responsible scheme of things. Reading back into this situation an adult's knowledge of mythology, you could say that my mother appeared as a chthonic Maenad in revolt against the paternal Apollo, with his rule of reason, order and light. And I myself was entirely on the side of the Apollonian angels.

Supposing now we switch back to the introverted interpretation. The normal boy's vitality is intensely masculine. But I was a good little boy, and not very masculine in type, anyway. The whole of my effective vitality—mostly feminine, but including a masculine component—was projected onto the figure of the negative mother, and then rejected. With such an appallingly dynamic skeleton in my cupboard, no wonder I wasn't particularly successful later on in making an adequate adaptation to life!

The dream itself didn't relate to the past, though the past had laid the foundations for it. It was extorted from me—wrung out of my psyche—by an acute conflict situation in the present. Except in its vibrant dynamism, the female figure wasn't like my mother at all. In appearance it was nearer to my wife. And my wife is the least demonic of women! In other words, the vitality and masculinity which had been wrapped up in the negative mother-image had now been transferred to my wife. But the net resultant in the psyche was not a portrait of anyone but a kind of mythological Gorgon.

We now come to the partial resolution of the conflict through the creative intervention of the shadow. On the face of it, there was something decidedly suspicious about the victory of the white god. A battle, even a battle of words, is not normally won by the overwhelmingly weaker party. In fact, the personality must have been able to detach a portion of the unconscious masculine forces from the demoness and transfer it to the white god's side. Then, *after* the event, this process becomes manifest in the emanation of the phallic serpent from the dark female to the light, masculine side.

The attribution of all power, including the phallus, to the Mother is, of course, a frequent theme both in individual analysis and in mythology. In mythology, it is the basis of the cult of the Great Mother. Also, in many myths, the overcoming of the archetypal, phallic Mother is the initial task required of the hero—*i.e.,* he has to reconquer his manhood from her. A beautifully lucid example of this motif is provided by the story of Perseus, who had to cut off the Gorgon's head—its hair a mass of writhing serpents— before he could be recognised as a man among men and win Andromeda (the anima) as his bride.

A terra-cotta in the British Museum depicts Perseus on horseback, with averted face, holding in his right hand the severed head of Medusa, the Gorgon. Out of the hole in Medusa's body, at the point where the head had been severed from the carcass, a slender naked form is emerging. This is the boy Chrysaor, who was born to Perseus out of the Gorgon's death. I find it impossible to avoid comparing this figure with the slender snake which emerged from the Gorgon's side of the quarrel in my dream. Both represent a slice of manhood reconquered from the negative Mother. I think my interpretation received further support from the myth of Perseus, which tells that Pegasus, as well as Chrysaor, was born out of Medusa's death. Pegasus, the winged horse, is quite obviously a symbol of masculine, instinctive power; taken in conjunction, Pegasus and Chrysaor would stand for virility in its instinctual and in its human form. The two aspects are combined in my dream, where the serpent of integration has a human face.*

No doubt it's inevitable to call the serpent in my dream "phallic." All the same, it's as well to bear in mind that it *is* a snake, not a penis. And my association to the young Jewish acquaintance whose face appears on the serpent's head is not potency in the sexual sense, but administrative competence and democratic—*i.e.,* liberal, Western—ideas. It's a case not of *savoir aimer,* but of *savoir faire.* As the dream image itself shows, it's a matter of phallic power in the *head.*

This brings us to the political aspect of the dream. It has to be remembered that I had this dream in 1948, when I was still at Wilton Park. At the time, I was acutely exposed to the onset of the Cold War, a phenomenon that had only broken out the year before. I was lecturing on the Foreign Policy of the Great Powers, and I had to deal, as best I could, with the occasional Communist in my classes.

*The statue is Terracotta 619 in the British Museum Catalogue; it is Greek, from the island of Melos, and dates from the fifth century B.C. For the psychological significance of Perseus, see the article on "The Psychopathology of Fetishism and Transvestitism," by Anthony Storr, in *The Journal of Analytical Psychology,* Vol. II, No.2, 1957.

The initial phase of the Cold War has by now been very largely forgotten. It's a fact, however, that the U.S. was at the period still dismantling its military installations and pulling back its forces after the war. Ernest Bevin, as the British Foreign Secretary, had his work cut out at one time to bring it home to the Americans that everything was no longer lovely in the garden. All energy and fulminating demonic power seemed to be on the Communist side during the period. The West as a whole hadn't woken up to the situation, and its policy was correspondingly fumbling and ineffective.

I myself was quite sincerely concerned about social justice, and was a moderate Social Democrat at the time. But this, to me, was an internal affair for Britain and for Western civilization as a whole. I was quite definitely committed to the side of the West. At the same time, I was very far from being sure of myself underneath. In fact, I was terribly anxious about Communism, which was making a truly formidable impact. It looked as though they might be too strong for us.

It's easy to see how this exterior situation came to correspond with the line-up of forces inside my own psyche. The airy, sketchily-outlined father and the raving, fulminating demoness of my dream fall neatly into place as Western civilization and Stalinist Communism, seen from my point of view at the outset of the Cold War.

XIX
A New Tack _____

The advice Jung had given me was definite and specific; in the circumstances, it would have been surprising if I had lost much time in acting upon it. So I consulted Dr. Gerhard Adler.

I was by no means disappointed by Dr. Adler. If anything, he was more Jungian than Jung himself. He told me I'd been lucky to "draw" Jung. He also gave me an interesting anthropological parallel to the quarrel in my Big Dream. Among some of the Eskimo tribes, there exists a kind of ordeal by slanging in which no weapons are used whatever, but words are hurled like missiles between the antagonists. The party who is silenced is subsequently killed.

Dr. Adler thought it would be a good thing for me to have an analysis with a woman; and he recommended his own wife, Mrs. Hella Adler. I accepted this idea with pleasure, and left feeling satisfied with my consultation.

Mrs. Adler — big, blondish and Mayfair — I liked and found attractive. She was a good many of the things I was not, and possessed a capability against which I could revolt. She belonged to Jung's school, of course; but the treatment struck me as very much like a competent Freudian analysis of a mother fixation. This was just what I needed.

My relationship with my new analyst was fruitful in a number of directions which started, but did not necessarily finish, in the analytical hour. For one thing, Mrs. Adler reactivated my swimming, and I'm always grateful to anyone who does that. In the second place, she introduced me to the Analytical Psychology Club of London, and in this way played the part of godmother to me in the Jungian movement.

No longer was I an isolated apostle to the gentiles, meditating on my own in the solitudes of Arabia. I had been brought into relationship with the Jerusalem Church. The effect on my life was profound and lasting — so much so that I have described the Club, together with its sister organization, the Guild of Pastoral Psychology, in a separate section.

Last, but far from least, Mrs. Adler asked me to write out my dreams and associations. This, too opened a new chapter in my life. I had done a little dream-writing before, for Dr. Laudenheimer, but this time I really took to the practice and built it up into a regular habit, which I kept going, with varying degrees of conscientiousness, for many years. The results fill twenty notebooks, some of them quite substantial, well-bound volumes; I keep them, if not at my bed's head, at any rate in a cupboard not far removed from it.

I think Jung is probably right when he says that the unconscious stands in a complementary or compensatory relationship to consciousness — the two together making up the light and dark segments of the one, single egg of wholeness.

When I talk about the *humorous* side of the unconscious, I mean it in all seriousness. One time, I remember, I'd been frightfully spiky and recited the entire office of Compline (in English) last thing at night before getting into bed. Next morning, a voice informed, with distinct emphasis, "I believe in the resurrection of the legs." If you *attend* to your dreams, you have a ready-made technique for correcting psychological imbalance. This process can be — and *has* been — compared to the automatic homeostatic balance mechanism that adjusts the temperature, etc. in the body, except that in psychological homeostasis the control may be at least partly conscious.*

I myself was not content with simple therapy. I conceived the notion of writing a Dream Diary. This was projected as a unique kind of psychological autobiography, to be recounted via my dreams. There was to be no continuous biographical narration; but if an incident in my life was called up as an association to a dream, then it might be recorded in literary form. So you got dreams and commentary, interspersed at intervals with some of the more lurid and emotional episodes in my career. The effect would obviously tend to be a biography whose materials had to some extent been preselected by the unconscious.

What the whole process did do for me was to give me regular practice in putting dreams and interpretations and gobbets of my life down in verbal form on paper. As I look back at it now, I can see that this sustained attempt at dream-recording put me through a kind of unconscious apprenticeship as a writer.

---

*There is increasing experimental evidence which suggests that dreams, whether interpreted or not, are essential to healthy mental functioning. If this is true, the parallel may be closer that I have suggested.

XX
Rival Gods _____

n 1950 I started to apply some of my insights to the psychology of the Cold War. I sat down and wrote an article some 2,300 words long. I hit upon the titles of "Rival Gods" for it. Here are some extracts from the article.

Rival Gods
by
Eugene E. M. Rolfe

From a purely economic point of view, President Roosevelt's dictum that there is no conflict of interest between the United States and Russia is as true today as when it was uttered... What is actually in progress is a war of religion. God is that symbol— under whatever name—which demands the total allegiance of man. In its purest form, the idea of Wholeness stands for that unified, total Self which both underlies and transcends the con-

99

scious ego and potentially includes within its scope the length and breadth and depth and height of which the personality is capable. Most frequently, however, the modern individual can only realize this idea in projection — ie., he discovers it embodied in some social ideal external to himself, such as Country, Leader, or Party...

The god which Soviet Russia has evolved is incomparably the most effective creation in this genre... Only those who are themselves blinded by the god or else by the superficialities of conscious rationalism can fail to discern that the driving force of Communism is a spirit...

When a new religion sets out to conquer the world, the course of history never does run smooth... But when the field is held by the figure of an established god, different but not extinct, and comparable to his adversary in psychic stature, a long, bloody, and possibly indecisive conflict may ensue, as at the Protestant Reformation.

As the image of the divine projection enters the field of battle, and god collides with god, the darker side of human nature, the Devil or Shadow, springs into view athwart the path... A creed that claims a monopoly of truth and virtue can only discern its own evil-mindedness in the figure of the hated, persecuted heretic...

While it is no secret that the god of Soviet theology has his holy mountain in the Kremlin, the devil, who in 1920 was an inhabitant of London, and in 1933 transferred his headquarters to Berlin, has since 1945 taken a pretty long-term lease of some desirable business premises in Wall Street, together with a holiday home at Washington, where he can relax at weekends.

The American god is a very close relation of the Russian devil — in fact, they have been observed walking arm-in-arm in the corridors of the United Nations. The American Mephisto, on the other hand — a red devil, if ever there was one! — is a prominent member of the Politburo in Moscow who is believed to have exercised a mysterious influence over the ears of Marshal Stalin. God, as he is know to Christians, has never been publicly disowned by American society; this is a factor of incalculable importance, since certain ultimate spiritual standards are still expected to apply, in public as well as in private life. But when we speak of the American god, we mean here what the average American would fight for in practice — Freedom, Competition, the American Home — the American Way of Life, in fact...

The Soviet god, impelled by the projections that cast America for the role of the devil in the drama demanded by the dogma of conflict, started the Cold War, and has maintained the initiative in it ever since...

The American god is at last provoked in reaction to the Russian, and the guns are being unlimbered and swung round outwards. Long before the Korean explosion, the proceedings of the House un-American Activities Committee had clearly shown how a divine aura was beginning to surround what is American as such, while the miasma of diabolism was seen as infecting whatever is unAmerican — i.e., Communist...

Never in the history of mankind has there been such a supreme need for cool, objective thinking — for the systematic, scientific study of the whole psychology of the other side — and that means, not merely what they will do but how they will be affected by our own conduct...

No god, however inverted, can successfully be opposed by a spiritual vacuum, even supported by tanks. What right have we to preach to the devotees of a modern idolatry if, with all our sanity and balance, our souls are full of emptiness, and there is no longer any room for a shrine? Where is the vision, the mystery, the living operative Truth, for which we would joyfully live and die, with all the strength of heart and mind and spirit? What is His name, my friend?

* * * * * *

The two antagonists of my Big Dream can be detected, not too heavily disguised, in the figures of America and Russia in this article. My Gorgon is included in the Russian god (I had often thought there was a primitive female quality behind a good deal of Communist propaganda, rather like the traditional male picture of the way a woman argues).

There is no feminine figure on the American side; and the Russian god is compounded with a Gorgon. This suggests, certainly in myself and possibly in the Western masculine world as a whole, an urgent need for the cultivation of a more positive relationship with Woman.

I hawked this famous article about on both sides of the North Atlantic for three years, without success. Finally, the Editor of *The Hibbert Journal* accepted it subject to certain minor alterations. And in April 1954 it was actually printed.

I ploughed my three guinea fee back into the enterprise by buying copies of the number containing my article, at the reduced rate allowed to contributors. I must have sent some fifty of these copies to prominent personalities of various kinds — Mr. Attlee, Arnold Toynbee, and Isaiah Berlin among them — as well as to personal friends and acquaintances.

Prominent among the prominences was Jung himself. It's scarcely a reflection on my other correspondents when I say that Jung's letter was in a class by itself. It was a single sheet, written on one side in his own handwriting throughout. Its text was as follows:

Prof. Dr. C.G. Jung   Küsnacht-Zürich
                                                       Seestrasse 228
                                                       May 1st 1954

Dear Mr. Rolfe,
    Thank you very much for your interesting article on "Rival Gods." Your ask a pertinent question indeed. I am afraid there will be nobody to answer it, as least not in the way, which we would expect following tradition. Can you imagine a real prophet or saviour in our days of television and press reportage? He would perish by his

own popularity within a few weeks. And yet some answer will be
expected. You rightly point out the emptiness of our souls and the
perplexity of our mind, when we should give an equally pat, sim-
pleminded and understandable as f.i.* Marxism. The trouble is that
most of us believe in the same ideals or very similar ones. Mankind
as a whole has not yet understood that the ultimate decision is really
laid into its own hands. It is still possessed by wrathful Gods and
is doing their will. There are very few who realize the true position
and its desperate urgency.

    I am glad you asked the question!

Sincerely yours,

C. G. Jung.

    I think that perhaps what delighted me most about this letter
was the proof it gave me that Jung was still in superlative form.
After all, he was now practically 79. And the firm, bold vigour
of his handwriting was coupled with an indescribable strong
rounded *fruitful* character, which I associated instinctively with
the female side — I could see at a glance that the feminine had
been integrated. It reminds me somehow of ripe, fresh pears, or
the flavour of golden, full-bodied, mellow wine.

---

*The letters "f.i." are Jung's personal abbreviation for "for instance," modelled, no doubt,
on the German "z.B.," for "*zum Beispiel*"

XXI
The A.P.C. and the
"Guild"

I n Spring, 1949, Mrs. Adler introduced me to the Analytical Psychology Club (A.P.C.) of London. This club had been founded in 1922 by a group of nine people, all of whom had had analysis with Jung himself.

I myself was not eligible for membership of the A.P.C. at this stage; I was, however, on the club mailing list from 1949 to 1957. This meant that I was able to attend Open Meetings, up to six of which might be held in a year.

I now heard a number of very high-grade talks, in which Jung's psychology was applied by experts to such subjects as "The Marriage of God and Israel in Ezekiel," "Man and Woman," "The Kabbalah and its Psychological Significance," "Waiting for Godot"—and so on.

I also got to know quite well (by sight at any rate) a good few of the regulars (both professional and lay) who constituted the Jung movement in London. Among the leading personalities I would include people like the late Dr. Leopold Stein (who knew Freud and Stekel in Vienna), the late Dr. Culver Barker, Dr. Michael Fordham, the late Mr. Philip Metman, the late Mrs. Irene Claremont de Castillejo and the Baroness Vera von der Heydt, as well as Dr. Gerhard Adler, whom I knew already.

Occasionally, a visitor from Zürich (where the C.G. Jung Institute was founded in 1948) would come over and read a paper. Dr. Rivkah Scharf, Miss Marie-Louise von Franz, and Miss Barbara Hannah were the ones I myself heard. Such a visit from G.H.Q., as it were, was an event to be looked forward to.

There are certain stories or types of material which positively clamour for a Jungian interpretation. The example which springs most readily to my mind is provided by a paper called "The Problem of the 'puer aeternus' in Modern Man (with special reference to *The Little Prince* by Antoine de St.-Exupéry)."* It was read by Miss Marie-Louise von Franz on July 19, 1951. The radiant clarity with which familiar figures like the Anima and the Puer Aeternus were exemplified, in this particular story, by the rose and the little prince himself, made occasions such as these the intellectual highlights of my life in post-war London. The theory slipped smoothly over the fingers of the facts — like some perfectly-fitting diaphanous glove, relating and illuminating but not distorting the material. Listening to a paper of this quality was like relishing the flavour of a vintage liqueur.

* * * * * *

In 1953, my family suffered a housing disaster. It was my fault really: to get to better quarters, I had taken a calculated risk. The risk came off; the calculation didn't. We were practically turned out into the street.

From the housing point of view, everything did turn out for the best, in the end. We bought a small house on a dying lease in Shepherd's Bush. Three years later we traded it in, as it were,

Puer Aeternus, Sigo Press, Boston, 1981.

and bought our present house, in St. Albans.

However, to get into the house at Shepherd's Bush, we had to mobilise every penny on both sides of the family. My share was a short-term mortgage. In itself, this was not an excessive amount; but it put off any prospect of analysis for the next two years or so.

In 1955, it dawned on me that I might qualify for membership in the Guild of Pastoral Psychology. I'd heard of this body before, but the Guild in the title had put me off: I imagined it was an orthodox, if not denominational, Christian fraternity—and if so, it was certainly not the place for me. But I was delighted to find that interest in the Guild's field or object (the common ground between religion and psychology) was the only qualification needed. The two dominant interests of my life which had met together in the person of Jung were also united in the society of the Guild. I joined, and became a full member.

XXII
Analysis or Life _____

T he possibility of analysis reappeared on the horizon as
our short-term mortgage sank gently to rest. That was
in 1956. As we had arranged, I got in touch with Mrs.
Adler and asked her if I could start again. She told me
she was too full up to take me herself, and advised me to choose
someone else from among the analysts I'd met at the Club.

It was a delightful and refreshing new departure to be handed
this complete freedom of selection. Never before in my whole long
and far from glorious career as a patient had I been in a position
to pick and choose my therapist.

The analyst I turned to was the Baroness Vera von der Heydt,
whom I knew not only from the Club but as Vice-Chairman of
the Guild of Pastoral Psychology. I see her as the fairy godmother
at the Guild. By birth German Jewish, by faith convert Roman
Catholic, by profession Jungian analyst, it was almost as if she
united in her own person the three great passions of my life. I

arranged to have a consultation with her. Vera von der Heydt saw
the problem very clearly. She knew about my financial difficulties, and told me that the mere thought that I had more money
now might itself ease my feelings considerably. When I told her
I felt I was still adolescent, she pointed out that this condition
was at least sensibly modified by my realisation of the fact. Finally, she recommended me to go along to the Middlesex Hospital, where I might get an analysis free of charge.

So my next port of call was the Middlesex Hospital (Department of Psychological Medicine), where I saw a senior consultant twice. The first time, a number of medical students were seated
around the periphery of the chamber, and I was the principal object of their attention. This appealed to the exhibitionist and to
the idealist in my nature. Was I not displaying my pathological
diathesis for the advancement of medical science? But a minority inside me, less conscious perhaps, rebelled and took umbrage.
I experienced this resentment in the form of a projection. "Other
patients" (I felt surprisingly strongly on this point) might be cut
to the marrow by this pants-down lecture-room exposure. I shud-
der to think what D.H. Lawrence would have said about it, for
example! Whatever else his mother-complex did to Lawrence, it
did *not* take away his aggression, his hate, and his power to protest.

At my second interview, (a tête-à-tête conducted along traditional lines), I was given my verdict. The consultant explained
to me in the kindliest way that *my* case was not really one in which
public money might justifiably be spent on an analysis. There was
an enormous number of patients needing treatment and, in the
nature of things, analysis could only be recommended for a very
small proportion of these. I quite saw the point of this assessment.

Though not as important as killer diseases, mental disturbances
of one kind or another are unquestionably among the principal
scourges afflicting our society. The Davidson Clinic (of Edinburgh)
puts it this way: "While it is well known that about fifty per cent
of hospital beds are occupied by patients suffering from mental
illness, it is not so well recognized that for every patient so ill as

to need hospitalisation there are at least nine suffering from some form of neurosis, while many others are anxious, worried, unstable or ill without any sort of diagnosis being made."*

My feelings of guilt would have made it completely impossible for me at this stage to accept treatment at public expense which I felt was in any way unjustified.

At the end of our talk, my consultant threw out a single, darkly luminous remark. He said, "What you need is a father-figure!"

I admit, this Parthian piece of advice did take me completely aback. It was like one of those uncanny, oblique strokes on the one weak, sore spot you'd forgotten. It had become almost second nature with me by now to envisage my problem as a mother-involvement; unconsciously, I'd let the *father* drop out of the picture. And yet, Lord knows, this father-business had played a big enough role in my story. Beginning with Eugene Alfred Rolfe himself, the line of these inescapable personages had continued, through Dr. Kidd, Father Maillard, and Dr. Laudenheimer, to the faint yet godlike father of my archetypal dream.

I could see the psychiatrist had got hold of something; and I dutifully rummaged around in my memory. Yet no very personable image presented itself as a possible candidate. Possibly some oldish minister at the Guild? Yet somehow I wasn't very hopeful about it. The blunt truth had to be faced: paternity was in short supply. Of course, there was always Jung himself—my spiritual father, if ever I had one. But he was far away, half a continent away, in Zürich.

---

*From "A Statement of its Purposes and Methods," a leaflet issued by the Davidson Clinic.

XXIII
Life

I t was in the autumn of 1955, as it happened, that I found myself a grass widower for a couple of weeks, so I reverted to my ancient haunts and habits.

I went to see one of my old associates from the days of the Bayswater Underground —Tony, the son of a former Austrian cinema pianist. I found a newcomer sitting on the end of his bed — a collected, rather hard-eyed and youngish man with a mop of dark, messianic hair. He told me he was living in Chepstow Villas, in what was apparently an empty house, where a number of people had taken up residence. A day or two later, I set out in this direction.

The place appeared in fact to be empty, and I walked right up the stairs till I came to the top floor. Here, I finally struck upon inhabitants, a slightly inchoate scatter of people, possibly seven or eight strong, of several shades of color and both sexes, most if not all of them younger that myself. They were not squatters, although in the absence of furniture they did tend to camp about on the floor. They were people who for one reason or another, either permanently or for the time being, had contracted out of civil society.

I spent several evenings in that vacant lot. On 26th August, 1955, when I went round again, I found the "occupied" house to all appearances unoccupied. As I retraced by steps haltingly down the darkened stairs, I was hailed by a voice from the basement flat. The voice came from Al, the young man who'd originally told me about the group; so I carried on downwards.

I found myself in a room which was comfortable and civilized, though bare. On the table were some paints, with which Al had been experimenting. Over the mantelpiece was a reproduction of the "Last Judgement," by Hieronymus Bosch. Hell figured prominently in the central panel. I translated the Latin inscriptions on this painting for Al, who (I thought) seemed interested. "The souls of the righteous are in the hands of God," they said, and "Lift up your heads, O ye gates, and be ye lift up, ye everlasting doors, and the King of Glory shall come in." I suggested to Al that the bestial bodies of the fiends and their victims, etc., were the appearance, in medieval art, of the animal, which had been repressed from the forefront of Christian consciousness. He said these things were more conscious in the East. I mentioned St. Paul—but the name was sufficient. Al chipped in immediately with "Not that he had any authority." I protested that he hadn't even let me finish my sentence; the quotation I had wanted to make from St. Paul ("Be not deceived. God is not mocked. Whatsoever a man soweth, that shall he also reap") was really in agreement with Al's own position.

I don't think my apologia for medieval psychology had been very much to Al's liking—even in the carefully qualified form in which I had made it. (*i.e.,* that hell itself as imagined by Bosch was marginally preferable to the total repression characteristic of bourgeois Protestantism). Had I also, conceivably, been a shade less than tactful in displaying my superior knowledge of Latin?—I don't know. But the fact is, in any case, that from that point in the proceedings Al and I became involved in an argument about religion.

I was sure that St. Paul did have authority and greatness in his own right, but the only way I could find to express this conviction was by saying that if it hadn't been for St. Paul Christianity would never have reached this country. Against this, Al maintained that Christianity would have reached England anyhow, and was in no way beholden to St. Paul's efforts.

The argument was now well under way, and at one stage Al challenged me by asking point-blank, "What is the heart and soul of Christianity?" I replied, equally directly, "The Holy Eucharist."

I'd now succeeded in annoying Al as much as he'd annoyed me previously, and he came back angrily with "Everybody knows the heart of Christianity is the way you behave to other people. It can't possibly be an external rite!"

I then proceeded to derive the Eucharist historically from the Passover (the barley-feast and the sacrifice of the lamb), and pointed out that the morning and evening prayer of the Church of England were descended from the old synagogue services, while the Eucharist continues the priestly sacrificial worship of the Temple at Jerusalem, the central service for every Jew in the Hebrew classical period. Al said Christianity had nothing to do with church-going.

My answer to this one was that the Gospels mentioned casually (and therefore not for propaganda purposes) that "on the Sabbath day, he (Jesus) was in the synagogue, as was his wont," *i.e.* that Jesus was a synagogue-goer. Al replied simply that Jesus "developed away from this."

This argument was a classic case — an absolutely priceless specimen — of an unconscious clash between the opposites, with incomprehension and rejection on both sides.

In our naive-mindedness, we always imagine that we can *eliminate* the opposite. That is the road to war (and the possible destruction of both houses). Love and sport and other sophisticated nominally unwarlike pastimes accept the existence and potential value of the other part and make possible a creative interaction between the opposites in which each side has the opportunity of transcending its one-sidedness.

Al and I were thoroughly naive-minded. The form of argument in which we had become involved is a struggle for mastery, not a search for truth. You could call it a kind of *wrestling* on the intellectual level, and it seemed to have brought Al and me closer together. We'd broken the ice with one another, and we felt more easy and relaxed. Al now volunteered to show me Soho. He took me to a coffee-hall called the Grenada, in Berwick Street, where I noticed (and admired) a big blonde woman, sitting on her own in a window seat by the door and industriously applying herself to the pleasures of eating. I called over to her, "Is it good?" and she called back "Yes!" with smiling gusto.

I'm not sure whether Al had a word with her, but all of a sudden, there she was, large as life, forging her way into the center of the picture and treating us both to coffee and cakes, which she interspersed with repeated handouts of King-Size Pall Mall cigarettes, built to the same ample specifications as herself. The question of entertainment — and of payment — for that evening troubled us no more.

It was a marvelous sensation of pleasure and wellbeing to be pampered and fed by this superlative she. She was so comfortably superior in size to the two of us that you could almost compare it with Romulus and Remus being suckled by the great she-wolf.

Very soon, we were all seated at a little table together, the blonde heroine and myself with our backs to the wall, and Al sitting opposite, to the right. I found I could talk (or rather listen) to her quite easily, without the slightest trouble or embarrassment, and we had a marvelous conversation, in which all the bars were down, and (consequently) not a single offensive word was spoken.

Her name was Rita, and eventually I found out that she weighed fourteen stone and was aged 42. She owned a great mastiff, the

darling of her heart, and with this rather awe-inspiring compan-
ion she used to roam the streets of London during the midnight
hours, visiting the Embankment and similar haunts. Rita and I
went on talking until half-past two a.m., when the joint closed.
Al and I then saw her home to her flat, which was practically next
door to the bar. But even now, our adventures were not over. In
a side street, a girl called out something. I turned back, and she
said "Come here!" In a moment, I was talking to a sizzling blonde.
As soon as she set eyes on Al, there was a cloudburst of recognition, followed closely by a waterspout of rapturous reminiscence.
It was an old girl-friend of Al's. A year or two before, she had
left Soho and migrated north. Now she was up here again, on
a visit — a sort of night-club queen on furlough.

She took a taxi, and we travelled back to Bayswater at her expense. And there I left the long-lost lovers — all that remained for
me to do was to walk the stretch home to Shepherd's Bush.

XXIV
Art _____

My reaction to the theological tussle was a very different story. I was *piqued* — really *touché,* exasperated and smarting — by my utter and complete failure to get my arguments about Christianity across. I really felt I was an authority on Christianity; it was my special subject, as it were — actually, one of the few subjects on earth that I could speak about with combined experience and knowledge. Yet what I said about it had been brusquely contradicted — just as though I'd been the merest vapouriser who didn't know what he was talking about. My expertise had been rejected!

Some of my colleagues at the office didn't seem to recognize me as an authority on religion, either. One of them, a fundamentalist, was an excellent Biblical scholar, and he backed up his prejudice with factual knowledge. It wasn't simply that he failed to grasp the symbolic significance of ritual: he rejected ritual out of hand, on principle. There was the same sort of "Shall!,"

119

"Shan't!," "Yah!," "Boo!" argument between us, neither side yield-
ing an inch of ground or conceding an atom of truth to the other.

There was a novelist, too, with whom I was acquainted (he is
now dead), a classical scholar and a rationalist, who could make
rings round me in any sort of factual argument. Yet he hadn't
the slightest gleaming of a conception of the importance of religion in human affairs!

The truth is, I was very bad at *argument,* by which I mean not
philosophical ratiocination or debate conducted according to rule,
but free-style wrestling on the mental level. I felt I was an
authority—like my father. *Unlike* him, on the other hand, I had
no schoolmaster's desk or platform to give my authority some
social backing. More serious still, I had no disciplined column
of controlled aggression at the disposal of my conscious mind,
which I could have used to enforce the recognition of respect,
if not of agreement, for my opinions. For a dogmatic authoritarian, I was terribly easy to brush aside. In return, I found it terribly easy myself to flare up and get frightfully hot under the collar.

I think it was the precise phrase "external rite," as applied to
the Eucharist by my friend and enemy, that provoked me to the
point of combustion. How anyone with inside experience of Christianity could possibly call the communion an *external* rite completely baffled my comprehension. Suddenly, a new resolve flashed
into my mind: "I'll jolly well show them—I'll write down what
I think—and *then* we'll see whether it amounts to anything!" Frus-
tration, by forcing me, at long last, to alert and mobilise at least
a portion of my essential resources, seems to have been leading
me towards, not away from, my essential self.

The title for the new book came to me almost immediately:
The Intelligent Agnostic's Introduction to Christianity. This title
shows clearly the type of reader I had in mind: an educated, lay
agnostic, brought up inside the Christian tradition and not actually antagonistic to the Church: someone not too dissimilar from
myself. The echo of Shaw was quite deliberate: I was conscious
of a slight thrill at my cheek in guying the great G.B.S., whose

vitality I admired but whose one-sided intellectualism had often irritated me.

On a piece of foolscap paper laid longitudinally, I mapped out a sketch or rough programme of my project:

(1) Psychological interpretation of "God"

(2) Consequences of the new conception:
  (a) morality
  (b) prayer
  (c) worship

The basic scheme or skeleton of this outline bears a suspicious resemblance to *The Idea of Humanity*. It looks as if I'm settling down to the game (by no means unfamiliar in literary circles) of devoting the whole of my career as an author to writing the same book over and over again.

Actually, though, eight years' water had flowed under the bridges since the time I made that first effort; and in two respects at any rate, *The Intelligent Agnostic* is a very different kettle of fish from *The Idea of Humanity*. In the first place, I'd absorbed a great deal of Jung's psychology in the interval. By now I'd made it so thoroughly my own that it had come to be the system of thought I lived by. So this time I made no attempt to impose the Christian doctrine of the family by force of argument. I kept strictly to my own experience of Christianity, and reinterpreted this by applying Jung's principles to it. As in *The Idea of Humanity*, I interpreted the first Christian commandment (Thou shalt love the Lord thy God, etc.) to mean "Be true to your own total Self." But I didn't try to derive the Second Commandment (Thou shalt love thy neighbor as thyself) from the first by dint of a chain of logical reasoning. Instead, I analysed conduct psychologically, in terms of the relation between the ego and the Self. "What the ego 'gains' by a mean action is a loss, not a gain, to the total personality." "Sin is essentially out-of-relatedness with God."

The second big difference between my two literary ventures was that the hot volcanic springs which were still seething when I wrote *The Idea of Humanity* had long since cooled down. By now, passion had become domesticated and had broadened out into marriage; the visionary insights of conversion had given place to the detailed labour of applying the "revelation" to daily life and making it available to other people. So while both books are full of argument, the *manner* of the second is far more measured and discursive, and far less like a mountain torrent.

In my section on prayer, I introduced a series of three very simple experiments, designed to enable the reader to decide for himself whether there is or is not any truth in the hypothesis that prayer can be a useful technique for mobilising the unconscious resources of the psyche and rallying them to the standard of the conscious ego.

I didn't claim either scientific rigour or religious sublimity for these experiments. What I did claim for them, on the evidential side, was a degree of pragmatic viability a good deal higher than that upon which most of our opinions and actions are actually based. And from the "spiritual" angle, I made the point that what has actually driven people into religion all down the generations has been, in the first place, the desperate need to get some help in the extremities of living. The desire to surrender our personal lives to the service of a power beyond ourselves comes later, if at all.

The organic, almost biological conception of God which I'd derived from Jung achieved an axiomatic formulation in the two definitions of religion which I gave in the course of a single paragraph. "Religion is man's systematic attempt to cultivate a positive relationship with life." And "Religion is man's attempt to deal with the unconscious." As a self-conscious being whose behaviour is not rigidly structured by instinct, man would appear to be the only animal who has either the power or the need to cultivate this kind of relationship. Thus defined, religion may turn out to be not a byway or an escape from life, but one of the characteristic achievements of humanity.

When I started writing this book, I had a considerable head of steam up. The writing bowled merrily along and I was surprised to find that the impulse lasted. True to my own nostrum, I prayed hard about it, and that helped to keep the kettle boiling.

The relationship of the new work to Jung himself might be said to be not so much simple as *duple.* In the first place, my faith in Jung was strong and untroubled. This was certainly an advantage; it made it possible for me to write freely and confidently, without being manacled by anxiety or doubt. The *thought* of the book — and the backbone of fundamental ideas behind it — is possibly 85% Jung and 15% other scholars and myself. Yet I shouldn't have a moment's hesitation in claiming it as an original work. The truth is that the application of Jung's psychology to the Christian religion as I knew it provided me with an almost perfect vehicle for the expression of myself. If the *thought* was his, the experience and the formulation of the experience in words were most decidedly my own, and that goes for most of the arguments and all the analogies as well. I didn't quote Jung once from beginning to end of the entire undertaking. And that brings us to the reverse side of the relationship.

The question of *acknowledging* my debt to Jung did exercise me a little. In *The Idea of Humanity,* Jung had been mentioned quite freely and openly, in the normal manner. But this time, I worked out a deep-laid and crafty stratagem. I was quite certain in my own mind that Jung's fundamental work — and particularly his discovery of the Self and its expression in the mandala — was of a revolutionary importance to the human race which put Jung fully on a level with Freud and Einstein, if not with Darwin; and that this epoch-making discovery — this Copernican change in both religion and psychology — had been allowed to pass almost totally unrecognised, rather like Mendel's theory of genetics during the first forty years after its original publication.

I was equally convinced that the disintegration of orthodox Christianity had laid bare man's ultimate religious need, which is just as real and in the long run more indispensable than man's requirement for sexual satisfaction.

Jung's discovery could of course help to fulfill this need. Yet the plain fact was that this discovery was just simply not being propagated. The reason for this sorry state of affairs was – or so it seemed to me – that Jung was dismissed off-hand as mystical, without being read, let along understood.

The project for *The Intelligent Agnostic* was actually based on a cool wager of intuition. I was prepared to back my own hunch that if the case for Jung could be expressed in clear and simple terms, fresh from the mint without benefit of jargon, in such a way that the stereotype "mystical" was not excited in the reader's mind, then a spark would fly over from the archetype in Jung to the archetypal vacuum in the reader, and the message would necessarily get across. And I believed that my book could do this job.

To quarantine this admirable design from the unclean miasma of mysticism, I hit upon the ingenious expedient of suppressing all explicit reference to Jung whatever in the actual text of the book – the idea being that my readers (who would, no doubt, be numbered by the millions) would be overpowered by the dazzling reasonableness of my exposition and would then subsequently tumble to the conclusion that my interpretation of Christianity was, after all, based on C. G. Jung.* In this way, the book's triple object would be realised: a sceptical public would be convinced of the psychological necessity for religion; the essential greatness of C. G. Jung would be recognised; and (last, but by no means least!) Eugene Rolfe would become famous as a writer.

---

*It is fair to add that I did include two of Jung's works in the Bibliography; in particular, it contains the unqualified assertion that *The Integration of the Personality* "records the most important religious discovery made in Western Europe since the Reformation."

XXV
The Holy Eucharist _____

The writing ran along pretty well according to plan till I arrived at the last item on my programme— "Worship." The rough sketch had listed this as co-ordinate with the other four sections—*i.e.,* approximately equivalent to a chapter. However, when it came to the point, I found that this concluding chapter completely shattered the scheduled framework.

Under "Worship," what I had in mind was a psychological interpretation of the Eucharist. This was the durable crystal which seemed to have remained among the clinkers of my dying passion for Catholicism. I was anxious that, if possible, all those years of experience shouldn't expire without contributing a crumb of comfort to somebody.

Every time I attended the Eucharist, I had the curious yet unmistakable feeling that something had been *done,* something had happened. Every time, before the service was over, I was able to repeat to myself the ancient Roman formula of dismissal, *"Ite! Missa est."* ("Go! It is a Mass.") By this I meant that the business had been transacted, the job done. But what was this business? I had no theological or metaphysical framework which could guarantee the efficacy of the sacrament from outside. In fact, my attitude could be described as experimental. I was prepared for the experiment to fail. Yet in practice every Sunday the experiment succeeded. What then was the meaning of this service?

I'd read Jung's essay on "Transformation Symbolism in the Mass," and this made it clear that the business which was transacted in the liturgy was essentially the sacrifice of the ego to the self. You could call it a mystery of transformation.

Now I set myself to work this out in my own way, in terms of the Old Testament prototypes and the New Testament documents, and I finally applied the results I had obtained to the text of the Anglican rite as I knew it. It was by far the biggest piece of research I had ever undertaken on my own account, and it filled up the whole of the second half of my *Intelligent Agnostic.*

XXVI
Publication _____

I 'd been writing into the blue for nearly three years now without the slightest guarantee of publication, and it was a wonder the impulse had carried me so far.

I was still fairly bursting with unlived life, and the book did restrict my leisure. Inevitably, I suppose, a remark I overheard to the effect that D. H. Lawrence's writing was an "escape from life" started a train of anxiety, guilt and doubt in the unconscious that nearly brought me to a standstill. I was still far from securely based; it didn't take much to undermine my confidence. Luckily I had a father-figure at the time in the person of Mr. Wyatt Rawson, the leader of a P. W. Martin Jung group in London I belonged to for a few months. I brought up my problem at the group, and Wyatt said that, as I'd gone on so long, I might as well persevere with my project. This timely advice just tipped the balance and gave me the encouragement I needed. I decided to carry on and finish the book.

I was now forty three, well inside the second half of life and within hailing distance of the masculine climacteric. From the worldly point of view, I was a failure. For me, it was a matter of life or death to achieve something concrete in the outside world. I felt obscurely that I must make a supreme effort *NOW—* otherwise the whole of my university education, my life's experience, my suffering and such insights as had come out of all this, would perish with me, sterile and unfructified.

On 18th January, 1958, I packed up the precious volume, and sent it off to Christy and Moore's, the literary agents. After about a month, I had a letter from John Smith, who told me that I'd written a "stimulating book" and that he'd be "delighted to try to place" it with a publisher. This was sweet—like a foretaste of paradise!

I'd picked up the idea from somewhere that an agent must on no account be pestered—that he must be allowed time to complete his job. I'd worked out that six months was the appropriate period, and I stuck to this programme in spite of the waiting. Then, at the end of it, I wrote in. John Smith told me in his reply that he was still doing his best to place my book. This (and particularly that little word "still"!) made ominous reading; yet almost immediately it was followed up by another letter, which informed me that Messrs. Skeffington, of the Hutchinson Group, were "very interested" in my book and were considering publication. This second shot was possibly the most glorious piece of news I'd ever received in my life—but unfortunately the agony was by no means over.

In the first place, the publisher suggested I might shorten my paragraphs (some of them ran on for two pages or more!). So I reparagraphed the entire book. The net result was sheer gain—a script that was lighter and more contemporary on the eye, and less like a history by Mommsen or a monument to nineteenth century philosophical verbosity.

I was also threatened, at one moment, with the excision of my priceless liturgical chapter—for me, very nearly the jewel in the casket. But I fought back. I put up a reasoned case for the retention of the chapter as an integral part of the programme of the book; at the same time I lopped off from it some initial portions which weren't really essential to the argument. Thus reduced, I was allowed to pass the barrier.

The way was now clear for publication—this was in November, 1958—but it wasn't until the following May that I was given an approximate publication date—31st August, 1959. At the same time, I received a polite request for the Index.

This was a feature I'd suggested myself—I was grimly determined to do what I could to ensure that my book should be taken seriously as a work of scholarship. But an innocent-looking little clause in the contract had stipulated that an Index should be prepared by the *author*—and in fact I did the whole job myself.

I was determined that the index should contain all important names and concepts, and these ranged from Plato to Pelmanism, from the Buddha to the Bomb. I worked from the page-proofs of my book. I prepared foolscap sheets for every letter of the alphabet, and methodically noted down all references with their page-numbers under each letter on the appropriate sheet every time they turned up in the text. It was excruciatingly labourious donkeywork, and to finish the job by the deadline—mid-June—was a completely and utterly hopeless undertaking.

But deliverance arrived from an unexpected quarter. The great printers' strike of 1959, which broke out on 21st June, knocked the bottom clean out of the August publication date, and brought me a reprieve.

At last, in my small, rather sub-standard existence, I had discovered an object of genuine concern—an object for which I was prepared to make real sacrifices. The concern, to be sure, was not purely disinterested, but how many genuine concerns are? My wife and I went on a two-week holiday to Westendorf, in the Austrian Tyrol. And there was I, on the balcony of the Hotel Post every morning, slogging away at my index in a grim, desperate and methodical manner! My sister-in-law, who had joined us from

New York, was quite impressed by this unexampled activity.

At this juncture, a new thought struck me. I'd hardly dared to expect (though I secretly hoped) that Jung would live to read my book. He was now very old (practically 84) — and yet, astonishingly, he was still alive. But of course, he might die at any moment, and now I was suddenly seized by anxiety that the wretched strike, which had deterred publication, might actually prevent him from ever seeing a copy.

So I wrote Jung the following letter, there and then, from the hotel in Westendorf:

Hotel Post, Westendorf, Austria.	as from 44, Brampton Road St. Albans, Herts., England

1st July, 1959

Dear Professor Jung:

I am sending you a copy of Skeffington's List for 1959, which contains an advance notice of my book, *The Intelligent Agnostic's Introduction to Christianity.* This was to have been published in August, but the strike in the printing trade in England will defer its publication, possibly for several months.

The book contains a record of a good deal of my experience, among other things, of the Eucharist. But your interpretations have provided the Richtschnur* which has enabled me to make some sort of sense of my experience.

The Church of England, that typically English institution, with its unique compromise between Protestant and Catholic, is typically English also in this, that it had devoted very little attention to psychology. The Roman Catholics have been far ahead of us in this. So far as I know, my book contains the first attempt to treat the Eucharist from the Anglican point of view along the lines of your psychology.

Another point is that I make no positive metaphysical assertions. I am just reading *The Paradise Tree,* by Fr. Gerald Vann, O.P. This

---

*Guiding thread

is an interesting and in places a beautiful book, and he quotes your works on "Symbols of Transformation" and on the Mass, but the standpoint of Roman Catholic orthodoxy is assumed throughout, and I personally find this a limiting factor.

May I say how keenly I enjoyed your latest book about "Flying Saucers"? It is beautifully fresh and contemporary in its approach, and made me, and I believe many other people, think furiously. I was particularly interested in your appeal to the churches to devote a little more attention to explaining religious matters to sophisticated people in the West, where you have to talk "up" and not "down." This is what I have tried to do in my book, taking particularly the ideas of God, morality, prayer and worship.

It is scarcely to be expected that my own curious psychological development has not been reflected somehow in my book. But whatever insight it might contain has come to me largely through your psychology.

It will give me very great pleasure to send you a copy if and when it does finally see the light!

Thank you once again for all the tremendous help you have given me.

> Yours sincerely,
> Eugene Rolfe.

It was an odd sensation sticking Austrian stamps on a letter from myself to Jung at Zürich.

This time, I didn't have to wait very long. Jung replied in less than a fortnight. The letter was typewritten, and filled rather more than half a page of the familiar, woven, headed notepaper.

Prof. Dr. C.G. Jung   Küsnacht, Zürich
                                       Seestrasse 228
                                       July 14th 1959

Eugene Rolfe, Esq.,
44, Brampton Road
St. Alban (sic), Herts.
England.

Dear Sir,
Thank you for announcing me your good intention to send me your forthcoming book *The Intelligent Agnostic's Introduction to Chris-*

tianity. This is, I hope, the book I am looking forward to. Theologians seem to be quite unwilling to take up their pen in favour of this subject. It looks as if they had completely lost sight of that audience which is not below, but at least on the level of their pulpit. The modern European however, is sick of being talked down to himself. It frequently fell to my lot, that I, being a mere psychiatrist, had to explain to my educated patients, that Christian religion is meaning something after all — a task the Theologians apparently have not recognised. Some new wine has been pressed since the middle-ages, but the Church still prefers the old skins. No wonder, that the spirit escapes and leaves the dead dregs behind itself. "Thou *must* believe or be damned," but, if possible, no religious experience please, as the truth has been revealed for all times and God is not supposed to be able to produce a new book after the original edition 2,000 years ago. I must admit however, that the conservatism of the Theologians is quite right, inasmuch as they have not yet thought enough about that, which they preach. I had to explain f.i. to a Jesuit father, Professor of Theology at Munich University, that in as far as according to the teaching of the Church, Christ and his Mother are not human, because not tainted by the *macula peccati.** Incarnation is incomplete. Christ was not born in a corrupt body, as Man is. This was news to him, because he had never given a thought to this question. This is only an example of several, which shows the regrettable absence of reasonable thinking. I am glad to know, that you found my Saucer-book enjoyable reading.

Sincerely yours,
C. G. Jung

I need hardly say, I was delighted to receive this amusing and entirely characteristic letter. It made me keener than ever to send him the book and to get his opinion of it if I possibly could.

When Jung says that man is born in a corrupt body, he is accepting Catholic doctrine at its face value for the purpose of his argument. His own position, as I understand it, is that man possesses a shadow, a dark animal background, a saurian tail — in fact all the potentialities which in our tradition are personified

---

*"The stain of sin", a technical term in Catholic theology for the taint of Original Sin. Hence the term "the Immaculate Conception."

archetypally as the Christian Devil. He also possessed the "good" potentialities which are personified in the figure of the Christian God. Good and evil are on this level relative terms. Both represent structural elements in human nature, and God and the Devil belong together to complete the pattern of totality. The Whole Man does not suppress evil, but lives creatively out of the ambiguous plenitude of his nature. By doing this, it can be contended, he in fact achieves a higher good.

Such people are rarities, but when they occur, they are very noticeably less boring than the conscience-stricken upholders of orthodoxy. And Jesus himself may well have been of their number.

The Catholic doctrine of Original Sin is a theological formulation of the psychological fact that we humans inherit a sneaking inclination to be bad. But if Jesus, in his capacity as the sinless Saviour, was, so to speak, immunised at source* from man's ancestral proclivity towards evil, then it is perfectly true to say that he was not fully human, and the Incarnation was to that extent incomplete. We are left with the image of the white castrato Saviour, and Jung's essay on Aion (*C.W.* Vol. IX, Pt. II) is an extended attempt to show that the traditional figure of Christ is an inadequate, because one-sided, image of the Self.†

To return to the narrative: the day came when my famous Index was actually completed and I dispatched it to Skeffingtons. It contained — after all the moil and pother — a thousand entries and upwards of four thousand references in all.

Meanwhile, on 5th-6th August, work was resumed after the great printers' strike. At the end of September, a note arrived from Hutchinsons announcing what proved to be the final publication date — 2nd November, 1959. The strike which seemed to have deferred publication to a completely indefinite and unpredictable future had in fact caused just over two months' delay. Yet on 22nd October an event took place which caused a distinct shift in the entire situation. This was nothing less than the appearance of Jung

---

*The dogma of the Immaculate Conception that Mary was conceived without original sin.
†Christ needed the AntiChrist, as God needed the Devil, to complete the circle of totality.

himself on B.B.C. Television, in an interview "Face to Face" with John Freeman.

In one respect, at least, the reactions to this interview confirmed my estimate of the position held by Jung and his ideas in England. A large section of the educated world was frankly taken by surprise by the discovery that Jung was still alive! Jung's appearance in person effectively demolished the assumption that he was long since dead. On the contrary, he proved to be very lively indeed! He became a vivid, actual personality for millions of viewers to whom the Big Three of depth psychology were no more than a legend, if that. In personal terms, Jung was now a figure to be reckoned with.

But Jung's dramatic reemergence had a rather chastening effect on my own pipe-dream that *my* book might turn out to be the chosen vessel for bringing his ideas before the educated public. After all, who could possibly be better qualified to put the case for Jung than Jung in person?

Nor is the point merely verbal. Jung was always at his best in a personal encounter. The wealth of his classical and other erudite learning, which makes his writings heavy going in places, didn't obtrude at all in the broadcast. And the intuitive immediacy of his approach was a decisive advantage in the live medium. The professor never stood in the light of the man. And the man—old, humorous and wise—was big—there wasn't a doubt about it, and he came across in a big way.

It took quite a while for the implications to sink in. But eventually, I did have to get round to the notion that, far from my book being a source of publicity for Jung, Jung was more likely to be a source of publicity for my book!

On October 11th, the *Sunday Times* published a photograph of Jung with a note announcing the forthcoming attraction. Jung was shown sitting up in a wicker chair, with his left leg crossed over his right. He was holding a walking stick in his right hand, while his left hand was up behind his ear, apparently to help him hear some remark or question. He was looking up in keen attention, and his mouth was slightly open.

It was an entirely informal snap, but I could have loved that man. There was a link of resemblance to my own father, who had actually been six years senior to Jung. There was such a stylishness about the old man, he was so "spry" (to use the *Sunday Times* word). And his face had that look of brilliance, vitality and fruitfulness about it which proclaimed how abundantly he had lived up to his name.

The broadcast itself was excellently staged. It was introduced by a kind of signature tune (actually, the Overture to Berlioz's "Les Francs Juges"), which had a swirling lilt with a dash of the military that was quite astonishingly evocative. While it was being played, the waters of Lake Zürich were shown on the screen, and floating on the waves was a small, rectangular piece of paper with the name C.G. Jung handwritten upon it. Music, and water, and the single, mysterious, fascinating name. Somehow, the combination transmitted a magically heightened sense of expectancy, of *occasion*. If the occasion was a confrontation with a genius, there was certainly more than a touch of genius in the way the program was introduced.

Like many other people, I was captivated by Jung's deep, powerful voice, and the charm of his democratic Swiss accent. It was subtly different from the German, and it had a touch of peasant simplicity about it. When Jung described how, before he became fully conscious of himself at the age of eleven, he had been living "in a mist," I was attracted and disturbed at the same time. I liked his voice and the way he said these words; but they also touched the chord of a painful association — the everlasting parrot-cry that Jung was a mystic. Well, here he was, living in a "myst"! This links up with his frank admission later in the talk, when John Freeman asked him about his own psychological type, that his relationship to "reality" had not always been of the strongest. Jung was an introvert, and he admitted it.

Jung's exploit as a boy, when singlehanded he routed no fewer than seven village lads who had set upon him all at once, was a very different kettle of fish. It was a perfectly marvelous story for everybody and it should, I thought, prove an effective counter to the myth of Jung as the airy-fairy dreamer, with his feet miles away from the earth.

Like everybody else, I imagine, I was attracted and gripped by the story about the incident at school, when the teacher refused to read out Jung's essay to the class, though it was easily the best, on the grounds that he couldn't possibly have written it himself. Here we caught a glimpse of the genius-child, of a type perhaps almost commoner among Jewish than among Gentile people. In fact, it reminds me of the boy Jesus confronting the doctors in the temple at Jerusalem.

I was pleased by Jung's modesty when Freeman challenged him to say whether he considered his psychology more scientific than Freud's. "I think my method has its merits," he replied. The philosophic tone in which he said this, and the complete absence of strident self-assertion seemed to me to be marks of an integrated personality.

I was touched by Jung's unyielding refusal to disclose the dreams related to him by Freud during the period of their mutual analysis when they were travelling together to lecture in America. On this point, I thought Freeman pressed Jung a shade harder than was strictly decent. Freud was dead: why shouldn't the dreams be told? But this was a professional matter; and here, Jung was the immovable stone. He took his stand on the law of medical discretion. Dreams told in confidence to an analyst are presumably just as sacred and secret as crimes revealed to a priest under the seal of the confessional. The death of a penitent or patient does not necessarily dissolve this obligation. And I thought that Jung probably also felt bound by personal loyalty to his dead colleague.

At the end of October, I received from Skeffingtons my six author's copies of *The Intelligent Agnostic*. One of these, without delay, I packed up and sent off to Jung in Zürich. I wrote a Latin dedication inside the cover, expressing my gratitude and filial affection. It was the kind of thing my father would have appreciated. Jung, too, belonged to the diminishing ranks of the same old classical fraternity, and it gave me a kind of conspiratorial pleasure to know that he would understand. Incidentally, I believe these two words, affection and gratitude, express the feelings of most English-speaking people who had any kind of personal contact with Jung in his later years.

I sent the following letter to accompany the book:

44, Brampton Road,
St. Albans.
30th October, 1959

Dear Prof. Jung,

It is with the greatest pleasure that I now send you—as I promised—a copy of my first book, *The Intelligent Agnostic's Introduction to Christianity.* I do so with the sincerest gratitude and affection, as your line of thought has continually inspired me since it first made its mark on me in 1946. In 1949, as you may remember, you were kind enough to read my MS *The God of Humanity,* and to send me your criticism and advice.

Although I still have some psychological difficulties, it is, I think, a measure of development that I have been able to write this book and get it published. The practice of transcribing and commenting on my dreams gave me a kind of apprenticeship in writing.

I was born in the fateful year of 1914, and I wrote the book in the evenings of September, 1955 to January, 1958. In a way, it is a kind of precipitate of my religious and psychological experience over the past 25 years, though I do not want to exaggerate the importance of that experience.

As you know, although there are excellent books about Zen Buddhism and other oriental religions, there still exists among educated people the greatest ignorance and incomprehension about the meaning of Christianity. And Christianity after all remains, if only negatively, still the effective religion of the West. My book is an attempt to *introduce* people to the meaning by an interpretation along the lines of your psychology. You will recognize your thought on every page; yet the *expression* of that thought is entirely my own and I have worked everything out in terms of my own experience.

This brings me to a point which does require a word of explanation. I do not mention you by name in the text, though the Bibliography contains a very plain reference. I need hardly say that this is not because I am at all reluctant to acknowledge my incalculable debt to yourself. Quite the contrary! The real reason is a deliberate decision of tactics. I am at present entirely unknown, and the educated public has no prejudice either for or against me. I shall not be dismissed *a priori* by an irrational projection such as "mystical." Therefore, my argument will, I hope, be considered entirely on its merits. If it is favourably received, people will then realize that the essential inspiration comes from you and the book will thus, I hope, be the means of introducing your psychology of religion to a wider circle of readers than might be reached by a book bearing an official Jungian "imprimatur"! At the same time, any defects in the presentation will be laid entirely at my door. I do hope you will forgive this innocent deception!

Freud's archetypal discoveries met the needs of the early twentieth century and have made his name a household word. But I have been strongly convinced for years that your own discovery of the archetypes themselves and above all of the mandala symbolism and the archetype of the Self are at least as significant in the long run as those made by Freud. And the need of the second half of the twentieth century is not so much for a negative stripping down of prejudice as for a positive guide to the meaning of living. Increasing numbers of people since the war have been finding this guidance in your own psychology. But the sharp decline in classical learning and also, perhaps, the almost total absence of philosophical training even among educated people in England have made your own writings less accessible than they ought to be. Thus, though there is an enormous need for your ideas, they are not getting across as quickly as they should to the thousands of people who urgently need them.

My book is an attempt to bridge this gap and to state the case in a popular, though educated, form. As you will see, it contains no technical terms in psychology, except a few that have already become part of our language — e.g. "the unconscious," "complex," "introvert," and "extrovert," and, sometimes, "libido." How far my attempt may have succeeded I cannot say — though, as this lengthy description proves, I have my full share of the author's normal tendency to inflation!

May I, in conclusion, say how very much I appreciated the interview you gave on B.B.C. Television? For me personally, it was the most important experience I have ever had on radio or television. A psychiatrist once told me I needed a father-figure. How great then is my good fortune in having found the most wonderful father-figure in the world! I have seen photographs of you but never before have I seen you so near to life — face to face! It was splendid to see you — if I may say so! — in such superlative form. Both your personality and your message came over magnificently. Today, more people than ever before are living into old age. Yet the Wise Old Man is an archetype which — it would seem! — finds no more carriers in our society. This rarity made your own appearances even more memorable.

I know of two women...both of whom appreciated you warmly. One was the neighbor on whose apparatus we saw you. She said that she would very much like to talk to you, and that she could learn from you, and she warmly agreed with what you had to say about old age and nature. The other...is a colleague of my wife's. She said she could understand you very well. Your English was both admired and liked.

On the whole, I think it is true to say that only a minority of intellectuals whose minds are clouded by the superficialities of conscious rationalism were unable to see you straight. All those who have retained their simplicity of mind — whatever their age, class or degree of cultivation — experienced no difficulty in "meeting" Dr. Jung.

With very best wishes and, once again, my sincerest affection and gratitude,

> Yours sincerely,
> Eugene Rolfe

There are traces of modesty, and even of honesty, in this letter. But these, surely, must be reckoned as dust in the balances compared to the cool, gargantuan effrontery with which I proceed to point out to Jung that, although I couldn't afford to allow my book to be contaminated by the smear of "mysticism" attached to his name, it was nevertheless my devout hope that this same book might prove to be the means of introducing his ideas about religion to a wider public!

Poor Jung! For about half a century he had had this beastly

taunt-word "mystical" flung against him with unending iteration. In fact, it had blighted his reputation and destroyed his effectiveness as a world influence in psychology. Yet he must have known that his contribution, in its different way, was as valid and significant as that of Freud. And he must have hoped that time and a gradual change of climate would finally bring about the recognition of his work that was its due. And now! here comes one on his side—and dishes up the same hoary old insult all over again! It says much for Jung that both book and cover letter weren't consigned to the waster-paper basket forthwith.

Three days after I sent the packet to Jung, the day itself arrived—the Great Day, the long-awaited—on which my book was actually published. I was keyed up to what seems now a quite ridiculous pitch of expectation—though at the time it was natural and inevitable enough. I dimly anticipated all sorts of reactions: for example, I was fully prepared for hostile criticism. But undoubtedly with the great event a kind of tremor would run through the universe. Nothing, thereafter, would ever be quite the same again.

I shall never forget what actually happened. For three or four days, in every direction, there was a total, absolute, deafening silence. I was like poor Scythrop (Shelley) in *Peacock's Nightmare Abbey* (a book, incidentally, I hadn't read at that time). In the cause of his "projected regeneration of the human species," he had written and published a treatise "which he thought would set the whole world in a ferment." He "awaited the result in awful expectation, as a miner who has fired a train awaits the explosion of a rock. However, he listened and heard nothing; for the explosion, if any ensued, was not sufficiently loud to shake a single leaf of ivy on the towers of Nightmare Abbey; and some months afterwards, he received a letter from his book-seller, informing him that only seven copies had been sold, and concluding with a polite request for the balance."

Meanwhile, another letter arrived from Zürich. It was signed by Jung's secretary, Mrs. Aniela Jaffé, and dated November 9th

1959:

> Dr. Jung asked me to thank you very much for kindly having sent
> him your book *The Intelligent Agnostic's Introduction to Chris-
> tianity*. He apologises for not writing personally, but for the mo-
> ment he does not feel well, and the doctor ordered a time of
> complete rest. He said he looked forward to reading your book,
> but this may take rather a long time. I hope that you will under-
> stand the difficulty of the situation.

This was grievous news! Once again, there was nothing for it:
I just had to possess my soul in patience. What I could do in the
meantime, I did. I replied to Mrs. Jaffé's letter. I followed this
up, shortly afterwards, by sending Jung a page which had been
shortened away from the liturgical chapter in my *Intelligent Agnostic*. It dealt with the influence of Zwingli on Cranmer. But I
also sent a note to Mrs. Jaffé in which I put things entirely in
her hands, since she would obviously know the right moment (if
any) to show them to Jung—the moment when, as I put it, "it
might cheer him up and not disturb him."

KÜSNACHT-ZÜRICH
SEESTRASSE 228

March 3rd 1949.

Mr.Eugene M.E.Rolfe,
19 Tremlett Grove,
London N.19.

Dear Mr.Rolfe,

I'm sorry to have kept your mansucript so long, but
I wanted to have it thoroughly searched, in which purpose I have
been helped by a friend.
The first part of your book is a quite interesting
attempt to apply the idea of wholeness to the individual in the
light of your own experience, but in the second part you fall
more and more a victim to the idea of a collective solution.
You say in your letter that you had a dream while
writing the first stages of your book, namely that you were
going to have a child, and that in the later stages you dreamt
that you had a baby, small but like yourself, and that at the
end you were afraid that it was a miscarriage. I'm afraid that
these dreams apply to your book inasmuch as the second part and
the end are premature attempts to translate your individual
experiences into a collective application, which is impossible..
You cannot teach a certain kind of morality or belief; you must
be it. If you are it, then you can say what you want and it works.
But you are not out of the wood yet. For instance, you entirely
neglect the fact that man has an anima that plays the dickens with
him - for instance, you married her - and the shadow rolled into
one. Under those conditions it is almost impossible to realize
ones own anima, because her reality is all the time right under
your nose and it is always pointed out to you that she is your
wife.
It is a great temptation in our days, when on talks to
Germans, to look for a sort of collective teaching or a collective
ideal, but you find only words that don't carry. But if you are a
really integrated personality, in other words, if you know all
about your shadow and all about your anima (which is worse), then
you have a hope to be the truth, namely truly yourself and that
is a thing that works. I could repeat the words of an early
Christian Papyrus which says: "Therefore thrive thee first to know
yourselves, because ye are the city and the city is the kingdom."
I should advise you to consult once Dr.Gerhard Adler
(29, Welbeckstreet, London W.1.) especially with reference to the
problem of shadow and anima.
I hope you will not mind the almost rude directness of
my letter. It is well-meant, as I know that if you should succeed
in publishing the book as it is now, it would be no success whatever, or it would have a wrong effect. I should therefore advise
you to keep the manuscript unpublished until the most important
question of the shadow and the anima has been duly settled.

Sincerely yours,

C. G. Jung.

The ms.is being returned to you
spperately.

V

Dear Mr. Rolfe,

Thank you very much for your interesting article on "Rival Gods". You ask a pertinent question indeed. I am afraid there will be nobody to answer it, at least not in the way, which we would expect following tradition. Can you imagine a real prophet or saviour in our days of television and press reportage? He would perish by his own popularity within a few weeks. And yet some answer will be expected. You rightly point out the emptiness of our souls and the perplexity of our mind, when we should give an equally pat, simple-minded and understandable answer as f.i. Marxism. The Trouble is that most of us believe in the same ideals or very similar ones. Mankind as a whole has not yet understood, that the ultimate decision is really laid into its own hands. It is still possessed by wrathful Gods and is doing their will. There are very few who realize the true position and its desperate urgency.

I am glad you asked the question!

Sincerely yours,
C. G. Jung.

Dear Sir,

Above all I have to apologize for the long
delay of my answer to the friendly gift of your book.
There is a history about it: It has reached me at
a time, which was the tail end of a series of
disappointments, which has brought me down
to the lowest ebb of feeling I ever experienced. The
evil thing was, that I had to realize the inability
to fight my battles anymore. I have to pay the
tribute to my old age and accept the beatings lying
down. I had to understand, that I was unable
to make the people ~~under~~ see, what I am after,
I am practically alone. There are a few, who understand this and that, but almost nobody, that
sees the whole. Your book now, which I am
absorbing with greatest interest, is like a ray
of light in the darkness of my time. But first,
when it came, I had to put it aside, because I was
afraid, it might be as offensively stupid, as all
the others. I gave it first to a friend to recommend it,
but before he could give me a report, I was caught
by a disease, which had me ad confinium mortis. Why
should I live any longer? My wife is dead, my children
are all away and married. I have failed in my
foremost task, to open people's eyes to the fact, that
man has a soul and that there is a buried treasure

VII

in the field and that our religion and philosophy is in a lamentable state. Why indeed should I continue to exist? A bad preparation of for a serious disease in my age! However I have picked up again and with that I could dare to take up your book again. I _was_ surprised. Since I have not finished it yet, I cannot give you my general impression. I only can tell you, that I am very pleased with your intelligent arguments. But if _they_ take you seriously, you will soon be in hot water. Happily enough — one could almost say — there are remarkably few minds today, which can take something seriously except themselves. Up to the present moment I am just grateful to you for your intelligence. It is after the floods of ignorance and stupidity I had to fight through, in itself beneficial and healing. I do enjoy your book. You are really concerned with the great problem, and not with the paltry interests of your academic career. You seriously want to put an end to the _trahison des clercs_ and you see Religion in its right proportions. Perhaps you can even explain to me, why people believe, that they possess a thing, when they have given a name to it. Primitives — yes, but that is why we call them primitives. Kant has never "x = placed "God (as I have not). His argument is merely: & Both Deus est — Deus _non_ est does neither affect his existence nor his non-existence, since est — non est is, as he says a mere "copula in the judgment" and not a magic formula. God "is a name, with which the Psychologist deals, and not a substance, the existence of which is not in question at all. Science is not Religion. Science has to be modest.

Yours sincerely C.G. Jung.

St. Albans Abbey from South West

GRANDHOTEL VILLA CASTAGNOLA AU LAC
LUGANO-LIDO

19 Nov. 1960

Dear Sir,

Having finished reading your book
from cover to cover I am now better prepared, to give you my impressions or rather
some of them. The Theme itself is so rich,
that one cannot hope to exhaust it.
I have discovered quite a number of old
friends in your book and I admire your wisdom and caution not to connect them with
my name of ill omen. I can say: you have
fulfilled your task to demonstrate the
approach to Christianity to a christian-
minded Agnostic. But if the latter should not
be christianminded; but thoroughly blackened

2. by the fires of Hell, which have been
thought in Europe since 20 years about
what then? It is beautiful to hear of the
Law of Yog-Asana, but what about the
Fear of God, the ominous message of
the Evangelium? ... ? Note to
Kant? ... oneword. The Apostles, far
days are by no means all Christianized.
There, at never, while goes much Yoga.
You call up again Tertullian's dictum
Anima of the first Roman centuries which
claimed the light, that relieth into the shed
ones. What about the Anima of our
benighted days? Let us hope that your
radius will find the way back to the past
of the centuries, the beautiful and spirit
gives baptized with fire mystery, the Eve
it and to fester emotions, the honorable
only the spiritual emotions. But
then the ominous history of the Jews will will
begin again with the fearful question of the

murderous darkness which complain
will not. The Sophiens of the priests here
is too obviously this.

By the way you seek the enigmatic
oracle "Vocatus atque non vocatus
abit" in vain in Delphi: it is cut in stone
over the roofing house in Küsnacht near
Zürich and otherwise found in Erasmi
collection of Adagia (XVIII Cent. Ed.) It
is a Delphic oracle though. It says: yes
the god will know the spot, but in what
form and to what purpose? I have put
the inscription there to remind my patients
and myself: Timor dei initium sapientiae
there another not less important road be
gins, not the approach to "Christianity"
but to God himself and that seems to
be the ultimate question.

Sincerely yours
C.G. Jung.

XXVII
Failure _____

Reviews of the *Intelligent Agnostic* now began to come in. The first words of the first review (it was in the *Herts. Advertiser*) read as follows: "A copious index indicates a scholarly approach." This was my reward — and I was amply satisfied! — for the hours I'd spent sweating on the balcony at Westendorf.

But what I was looking out for in my naive self-confidence was the double-column reviews in the Sunday papers. Every week I bought a *Sunday Times* and an *Observer,* and every week I drew a blank and felt a corresponding blankness of disappointment. My publishers explained to me most carefully that reviews of religious books were always tardy in arriving; all would come right in the end. And in fact, within four months of publication I had received fourteen notices; five more followed in the next four months making the total nineteen in eight months. Considering the type of work I'd written, this wasn't at all bad going.

Looking back in objectivity, I can't see that I had a great deal
to complain about. But at the time, I was strung up on a clothes-
line of anxiety. The waiting was almost unendurable. My great
project really seemed to be threatened with failure.

I sent out something like a dozen copies of my *Agnostic* to as-
sorted eminences in the literary world, etc.—over and above the
copies I was giving my friends. It was a self-regarding form of
generosity, no doubt. A young poet I knew certainly had a point
when he told me, "Well, it's your child—so you're naturally not
going to let it starve!"

On the whole, though, the critics were reasonably kind to me.
Nine of my notices were mixed or neutral, seven decidedly favourable and only three completely "anti." The seven "pros," which included the *Daily Telegraph*, the *Yorkshire Post*, and the *Times
Literary Supplement*, all appeared in secular publications; two
of the three "antis" were in religious papers. This was fair enough.
Apparently, I might get through to *some* of my agnostics. Orthodox Christians, on the other hand, could hardly be expected
to take very kindly to a rival firm's interpretation of their
doctrines—though several of them, writing in *secular* journals,
said surprisingly positive things about my offspring.

In a way, though, my anxiety did turn out to be justified. I'd
imagined that it might be frightfully difficult to find a publisher
who'd *accept* my book, but that, once published, it would have
been an immediate and overwhelming success. Almost the opposite proved to be the case. Not one of the quality Sunday newspapers or the fashionable political-cum-cultural weeklies took the
slightest notice of my prodigy. Yet the middle-class readers who
buy hard-cover books choose their titles from a list preselected
very largely by these papers. If a book is not mentioned in this
list, potential buyers will never have heard of it. Nor are book-
sellers likely to display it in their windows or on their tables.

It is true I did have one first-class review in a national daily
(the *Telegraph*) with a circulation of over a million. But this notice (three lines long), appeared with eleven other titles, in two

half-columns headed "Advent Reading"! Offhand, I couldn't think
of anything *less* likely to attract the kind of agnostic I was writing for. It is a rare event for a book classified as religious to break
through the ghetto walls and burst out into the secular sunlight.
My first-born, though addressed to the secular reader, did *not* come
into the dam-bursting category.

Of course, I could console myself with the reflection that I had
achieved a *succès d'estime.* My old friend, the *Hibbert Journal,*
with its international reputation in the field of religious scholarship, had awarded me their first review — almost two whole
pages — and had treated me with a seriousness that surprised me.
This, and the kind words spoken by the T.L.S., were enough in
themselves to guarantee respectability at any rate to my *Intelligent Agnostic* — at a level far above the sordid depths where sales
and readership made any difference.

This meant quite simply that my book had failed. It is true that
the respectable ghost of success made it suitable for purchase by
public libraries; and one way or another, I received enough letters from appreciative readers to reinforce me in my conviction
that it did meet a real need.

In August, 1960, Macmillan of New York bought nearly half
the original impression of two thousand, and this ranks as an
American edition — another corner-stone of the *succès d'estime.*

Eventually, the London edition quietly disappeared, and the
book slipped noiselessly out of print. It had not been remain-
dered, at any rate. But my *Agnostic* had been designed to go off
with a bang. It was deliberately constructed to provoke
controversy — and it had failed to secure the attention of the public.

This crucial failure struck me amidships, somehow, like a blow
on the psychological solar plexus; I sank down, down to the water-
logged bottom of a long, low, gloomy depression. I'd put all I'd
got into that book; and nothing, really, had come out of it. I'd
believed in the book with perfect sincerity; but I'd also believed
in its success — and mine! — and I'd wanted and needed that success very badly.

I think that what lowered me more than anything else was the painful, almost traumatic realisation that the launching of my supreme effort in print before the public hadn't altered my *real position* in the slightest. I was miserably starved for recognition. Nor was this surprising: my normal work didn't allow my peculiar talents to flourish, and I wasn't particularly forthcoming in personal relationships, either. If you don't pay attention to other people, you can't complain if they don't pay attention to you. But now that I'd made a serious contribution that really did deserve some notice, no more notice was in fact taken of it—or me— than before. I simply was not recognized as a writer.

Recognition, as I see it, is a universal and perfectly normal human need. In one form or another, we all have to have it. But to get it, you need to study the rules of the game.

Broadly speaking—unless you happen to be national figure— you can only expect recognition as a writer in England inside your chosen faculty or field. Admittedly, the house journal of the Ministry of Labour had given my book a most perceptive write-up. But that was a windfall, an act of grace—the exception which proves the rule. My topic was miles away from their beam. Recognition is in these cases very largely a function of the work situation. And the plain truth was that I wasn't *working* inside my chosen field or faculty. How, then, could I expect to find recognition?

But I wanted more than just recognition. Somewhere, deep down, I must have hoped very strongly that the book would somehow open a door for me—that it would release me out of my narrow little rut into a larger, fuller, freer life, in which I should be able to work creatively. I was asking my book to *carry* me into my true vocation.

But if success is in some way correlated with life, may not failure be similarly interwoven with death? Death and success! What a confrontation of opposites! When I think of it, I cannot help being reminded of that profound and foreboding remark of Adler's which had tolled a bell of warning inside me when I'd heard it, twenty-five years or so previously: "When the possibility of success disappears, the possibility of death appears."

In those days, the possibility of success was a vivid lodestar on the horizon. But the alternative had by no means been eliminated, either. Death was always possible if I failed in the contest. Both success and death, in fact, were potentialities deep-rooted in my nature; that is what made Adler's saying so poignant to me.

Since then, I could claim that I'd shed neurosis, in the sense of a virulent psychic anti-body that made life intolerable without treatment. Yet I'd never really managed to kick clear from the entangling *situation* neurosis had landed me in; I was like a snake imprisoned in its old skin.

Outwardly, my life went on much as usual. But inwardly, I was almost in despair. When my publisher asked me what I was going to write next, I simply couldn't answer. I'd no more ammunition left; my bolt was shot, my force was spent. And there was more to this exhaustion than the normal flop-back after a long period of extended effort. If my first shaft had manifestly penetrated the target, I should have felt very differently about following it with a second. As it was, the blank I scored knocked me out. The possibility of success had disappeared. Might not the possibility of death be appearing?

But what does "success" actually mean? It means, paradoxically, among other things, that for survival, *more* than survival is needed. This can be demonstrated with diaphanous clarity on quite a simple biological level. Put a large fish into a small tank and, though oxygen, food and temperature may be right, in a surprising short time that fish will be dead. Cut off the whiskers of a wild rat, and the rat too is likely to fade away—though he may be well supplied with the necessaries of life.* Without some measure of free functioning—the ability to *perform* as a fish or a rat—life is literally not worth living, and the creature pines away and dies. Survival, as I said, is not enough. *Biological success* may be a necessity of life.

---

*See "Anxieties about Life and Death," by A. Jores, M.D., in Spring 1961 (published by the Analytical Psychology Club of New York)

It is true that man is quite a complicated animal — far more complicated, for example, than a fish. A fish has his way of life built into him by nature: a man has to choose and achieve his own way. By the same token, man has far more compensations and substitutes open to him than are available to the poor thwarted fish in the tank. Delinquency, neurosis, depression, drinking, drugs — all these and a host of physical ailments are methods of keeping alive used by people who have lost, or never found, their own way in life. Death, whether by pining or by active suicide, is only the final throw that terminates the game.

Yet at bottom, man is a vital organism like the rest, and the law (if it is a law) will still apply. In fact, I suspect that the criterion of success (or failure) can be formulated in very much the same terms in the case of man, rat or fish — namely, "Is he living his own life in his own way? Or is his vital self-expression so essentially frustrated that life for him is not worth living?"* It could be argued, of course, that from the vocational point of view, *The Intelligent Agnostic* had at last annulled my bar sinister; after ten years' disqualification as a civil service minion, I was again in the running for a professional appointment.

I did argue along these lines; and, in fact, I did apply for a "supplementary interview" at the N.I.I.P. — a service which (for a very minor charge) remained open to previous recipients of vocational guidance.

This time, I saw a woman vocational officer, younger than myself, intelligent, and very sympathetic. She agreed that the *Agnostic* had altered my chances, and suggested I should try out a completely new line — technical magazine editing, for example. I should make a real *assault* on the problem. What I needed was a new experience — that was why I'd got stuck in my writing.

Her friendliness touched me and encouraged me. In the subtlest way, she had contrived to give me the impression that she

---

*The distinction, peculiar to the human species, between "true" and "false" (or "worldly") success might be explained by the following hypothesis. "False" success is the triumph of the ego; "true" success is the realisation of the Self.

thought me an interesting man. This was water to a parched land! It was far more precious to me than any fee I had to pay or any vocational guidance she had to offer.

She'd made two perfectly valid points, though, when she spoke about the need for assault and experience. I felt their applicability to myself—that's the only reason why they lodged in my memory. But to act on them was easier said than done. A new experience can't simply be whistled up out of the wind. And for an assault, a compelling motive is needed—particularly if you happen to be an indolent stick-in-the-mud whose not very ample stock of aggression is mostly repressed, anyhow.

Part Three:

Meeting

XXVIII
Waiting _____

Meanwhile, what about Jung? In January, I noticed a long letter to *The Listener* from the pen of C.G.J. himself, explaining what he meant by "God." He'd had so many enquiries about this question from viewers who'd been provoked by his cryptic utterance on television: "I don't have to believe: I know." On the same day (21st January, 1960), an interview he'd given Hugh Charteris appeared, excellently presented, in *The Daily Telegraph*. It was vivid, humorous, and altogether characteristic. Evidently the old man was in circulation again.

Eventually, in early April, I wrote to Zürich. I sent Jung the *Hibbert Journal* review, and told him that Macmillans of New York might bring out an American edition. I also told him that a well-known London analyst, Mr. Philip Metman, had liked my book.

And now, once again, I had to contain my soul in patience,

153

a most admirable discipline, really, if you don't happen to expire along the route. I waited another six months. It was in October, 1960, that Barbara Hannah (who was, as I knew, a member of the inner circle) came over from Zürich to give a lecture to the Guild on "The Religious Function of the Animus in the Book of Tobit." The talk itself was pure vintage Jung, and I savoured it like a connoisseur on a teetotal diet. I also appreciated the attractive aroma of the personality by whom it was delivered — the delightful, spontaneous, almost peasant wholesomeness of Miss Barbara Hannah herself. She too, like a noble wine, had mellowed with the years.

After the discussion, I made my way to the front, and asked Miss Hannah about my book. She responded instantaneously, with a keen vivid interest, and actually continued attending to me in preference to another questioner, whom she deferred. I was taken aback by this most-favoured treatment. Obviously, this was a matter of vital concern.

She listened carefully to what I had to say, and then she asked me, "So, you would like me to poke about a bit?" (*i.e.*, to draw Jung's attention to my book). I replied, decisively, "No! I *don't* want that. What I *would* like is if you could tell me when would be a good time to write." "Well," she said, "he's not allowed to deal with his correspondence at present. But write in about a month's time. Then it will be all right."

I need hardly say that I accepted her advice and fulfilled it to the letter. I told Jung about Barbara Hannah, mentioned that Macmillan of New York had now bought a thousand copies of the *Agnostic,* and underlined how invaluable his opinion would be to me, etc.

But this time, I also talked a little to Jung about himself. Apart from "heart-felt good wishes for a thorough-going recovery and many more years of fruitful life," I told him I had recently read, and since bought, Vol. IV, Part I of his *Collected Works (The Archetypes and the Collective Unconscious).* I went on to say: "I found the series of 24 illustrations, in the most beautiful rich colours, of mandalas painted by your famous woman patient a most satisfying addition to the literature. No one whose mind is not already possessed by hostile preconceptions can fail to be profoundly impressed by this sequence.

"Dare we hope that you have still not said your last word, and that this magnificent and truly worthy edition of your *Collected Works* is even now uncompleted?"

XXIX
Fulfilment _____

I had very little longer to wait, now. Finally, one morning, I received a letter from Jung dated 13th November, 1960 — the 21st anniversary of the beginning of my analysis at the Tavistock Clinic. It was closely written on both sides of one of the familiar large sheets of notepaper — entirely in Jung's own hand. The familiar writing, with its pointed brilliance, its vigour, and its indescribable quality of fruitfulness was still there, too; only this time it looked somehow broken. The letter ran as follows:

Prof. Dr. C.G. Jung,   Küsnacht-Zürich
                                        Seestrasse 228
                                        Nov. 13th 1960

Dear Sir,

Above all I have to apologise for the long delay of my answer
to the friendly gift of your book. There is a history about it: It has
reached me at a time, which was the tail-end of a series of disappointments, which has brought me down to the lowest ebb of feeling I ever experienced. The evil thing was, that I had to realize the
inability to fight my battles any more. I have to pay the tribute to
my old age and accept the beatings lying down. I had to understand, that I was unable to make the people see, what I am after.
I am practically alone. There are a few, who understand this and
that, but almost nobody, that sees the whole. Your book now, which
I am absorbing with greatest interest, is like a ray of light in the
darkness of my time. But first, when it came, I had to put it aside,
because I was afraid, it might be as offensively stupid, as all the
others. I gave it first to a friend to reconnoitre, but before he could
give me a report, I was caught by a disease, which led me *ad confinium mortis.** Why should I live any longer? My wife is dead, my
children are all away and married. I have failed in my foremost task,
to open people's eyes to the fact, that man has a soul and that there
is a buried treasure in the field and that our religion and philosophy is in a lamentable state. Why indeed should I continue to exist? A bad preparation for a serious disease in my age! However
I have picked up again and with that I could dare to take up your
book again. I *was* surprised. Since I have not finished it yet, I cannot give you my general impression. I can only tell you, that I am
very pleased with your intelligent arguments. But if *they* take you
seriously, you will soon be in hot water. Happily enough—one could
almost say—there are remarkably few minds today, which can take
something seriously except themselves. Up to the present moment
I am just grateful to you for your intelligence. It is after the floods
of ignorance and stupidity I had to fight through, in itself beneficial and healing. I do enjoy your book. You are really concerned
with the great problem, and not with the paltry interests of your
academic career. You seriously want to put an end to the *"trahison
des clercs"* and you see Religion in its right proportions. Perhaps
you can even explain to me, why people believe, that they possess
a thing, when they have given a name to it. Primitives—yes, but
that is why we call them primitives. Kant has never "exploded" God
(as I have not). His argument is merely: Both Deus *est*—Deus *non
est* does neither affect his existence nor his non-existence, since *est-*

---

*To the brink of death

non est is, as he says a mere "copula in the judgement " and not a magic formula. "God" is a name, with which the Psychologist deals, and not a substance, the existence of which is not in question at all. Science is not Religion. Science has to be modest.

Yours sincerely,

C. G. Jung

I read this letter, scarcely knowing what I read. Slowly, the meaning of it sank in. It was the most tremendous and overwhelming letter I had ever received in my life.

I had hoped for some friendly but detached comment on my *Agnostic;* that the book should have meant something to Jung personally went clean beyond my wildest dreams. The great scientist whose work had brought new meaning into my life had in some way been helped by what I had written. To talk of merit or deserving is ridiculous in such a case. It was a king of uncovenanted mercy—that was the phrase I used to describe it. I could only think that it might have been given to me because—through no virtue or demerit of my own—I had been through a certain amount of suffering.

I had already had some experience of Jung's directness. But this time, his frankness about himself was simply staggering. I could well imagine that he might not have felt free to write in these terms to a professional colleague. Instead, he had chosen to confide in me. My book (or a part of it) had in some way touched him; and, being an utterly genuine person, he had responded immediately, from the heart.

I was amazed, too, to find that he was passionately concerned and involved with the world, and capable of experiencing the bitterness of disappointment. The writings do not always betray the man. I'd been reading his books with enthusiasm for years before I began to get the glimmerings of an inkling (from people who'd met him—not from his works) about the extraordinary kind of *person* we had to deal with. It seemed that Jung actually felt, as I did, that his work had somehow never got through to the public. This was one of my leading ideas, and his poignant expression of it in the letter moved me indescribably, and drew me towards him.

Jung was behaving spontaneously—that was obvious; he was not setting out to cure me in any way. Yet what was the *effect* of the spontaneous reaction of this extraordinary, creative personality? It struck me directly, straight to the heart; it challenged me almost bodily, at the centre of my being. I was faced with something tremendous which I couldn't evade; I had to respond to it. For better or for worse, moral indignation at the wrongs suffered by other people is not the most salient characteristic of my psychology. Nor can I preen myself that this is a mark of maturity. A large part of the libido which should be disposable abroad is needed at home for the urgent task of protecting my own dear priceless little ego. But this letter from Jung pulled me right out of my defenses. It really roused my honest ire. When he spoke about his "inability to fight my battles any more" and of the "floods of ignorance and stupidity I had to fight through," what struck me was an indignant feeling of outrage that a man as old as Jung and as great in achievement should be *required* to do any such thing. What barbarity! I felt a native swelling of anger against the perpetrators—who were these persons unknown? I hadn't any detailed information about the "disappointments" Jung mentioned—but I could hazard a guess about one or two of them. Probably some of the letters he'd received after the TV appearance had something to do with it, I thought—that, and at least one recent book I knew of.

For years I'd been riled at the repeated cheap sneers at Jung in the fashionable intellectual press. I'd even written a massive epistle to a Sunday newspaper complaining about it. It almost seemed as if the crude jab at Jung had become a kind of ritual act in the anthropology of the cultural establishment. Jung was a *heretic*—that is, a man whose truth the ruling attitude was forced to reject.

Jung himself had been living with the fact of his rejection for the greater part of his working life—ever since his break with

Freud, forty-seven years previously. Almost all his pupils had left him at that time, and he had lost his position as a world leader of the psycho-analytical movement. He had had the enormous courage and endurance to stand alone and go his own way through the whole of this long period. Except for his wife and a handful of followers, he was totally unsupported. For the educated world of the West, Freud's psychoanalysis reigned supreme and was for several decades identified with psychology. All the same, by the end of the Second World War, there was a distinct shift in the climate of opinion. Psychoanalysis (deservedly) had come to stay. But in England, at any rate, the *craze* for it had blown over, and it no longer monopolised the public image. There was room for other insights in psychology—and even for other schools of analysis.

The Society of Analytical Psychology (the professional association of Jungian analysts in Britain) was incorporated in London in 1946. It became the largest group of Jungian analysts in the world. In 1948, the C. G. Jung Institute was founded in Zürich. There were similar developments in the United States. In 1953, the first volume of the great edition of the *Collected Works* of C. G. Jung was published in London and New York, under the joint editorship of Gerhard Adler, Michael Fordham and Herbert Read. The *Journal of Analytical Psychology*—international, professional, twice-yearly, and London-edited—started publication in 1955. In 1958, the first international Congress of Analytical Psychology was held at Zürich. It was attended by ninety-six qualified analysts and fifty-seven guests (mostly senior trainees; they came from Britain, France, Israel, Italy, Switzerland and the United States, among other countries).

Jung himself took little part in this series of quite considerable organisational achievements, which put analytical psychology firmly on the map and made it a force to be reckoned with in the post-war world. Though personally active and productive right up to the end of his life, he had always disliked and distrusted organisation, and he had never desired "to found a move-

ment." He had been surprisingly successful in this negative ambition. Otherwise, many of the developments outlined above might
well have taken place years previously.

Jung had long since retired from analytical practice. But he continued to preside as a father-figure—commanding, ironic and
slightly detached—over the expansion and consolidation of analytical psychology. And he may have felt (in the light of these developments, and for other reasons) that his ideas were now making
a considerable impact, and that the wall of blank incomprehension which had surrounded his thought for so many years was
at long last beginning to crumble.

The reactions to his television broadcast (among other things)
must have come as a profound shock. Many of his new correspondents, I would imagine, showed not the faintest twinkle of a notion about "what he was after"; and this must have brought home
to Jung the sorrowful reality that, outside a small circle of cultivated professionals, his lifetime's achievement in analysis and formulation was *still* largely unknown, or disregarded. So it is
understandable that in his nadir moment of depression, he should
have thought, "What is the use of going on living?" Yet to me,
even his despair had a creative outcome.

Jung's letter did more than raise my moral hackles in revolt
and indignation on his side. It raised something else inside me—
something which my tortuous psychological development had
made frightfully sticky and difficult for me—and that was the capacity to express my love.

Jung's amazing frankness had put the relationship onto a different, quite firmly personal, footing. It was as if a great wave of
love and sympathy was carrying me bodily towards him; and I
expressed all this, as well as I could, in my answer to his letter.
I wrote it, if I remember rightly, when I was confined to bed with
a chill.

I began by telling Professor Jung that his letter had brought
me great happiness and great sadness at one and the same time.
I went on to say how very much his kind words about my book

had meant to me.

   I continued:

    I have the very greatest sympathy possible for what you tell me about your feelings. Without the slightest point of comparison between myself and your own long life, crowded with work and creative achievement, I can at least say that *my* life has abundantly taught me what disappointment, long drawn out, can mean.

    When you write, "I have failed in my foremost task, to open people's eyes to the fact that man has a soul and that there is a buried treasure in the field...," I am unable to avoid thinking of the verse in St. John: "And the light shineth in the darkness, and the darkness comprehendeth it not."

    This it was already possible to say when the author of the Fourth Gospel was writing — perhaps shortly before the end of the First Century A.D. Indeed, it seems to me terribly possible that Jesus himself, the human figure who was called upon by destiny to shoulder this transpersonal burden, already believed when he gave that last dreadful cry of despair from the cross, that the light which he died to bring to men was being quenched in blood and darkness. Now however, looking back over to many centuries, we can surely say that through Christ a great light did burst on the world and did transform the course of human history. Please forgive me for even suggesting this comparison.

    You have always, with perfect consistency, "declined with thanks the honour" of being the Medicine Man, the Saviour, etc. etc. etc. But even an ordinary, second-rate person (such as, for instance, myself) may, in certain circumstances and to some extents, have the role of hero thrust upon him. You, however, Professor Jung, are in a different category. You are, if you will permit me to say this, of the stuff heroes are made of. And it does seem to me that destiny has laid a heroic burden upon your shoulders in quite an unusual degree. As I see it, your unique position derives from this: alone among Western scientific discoverers, you have brought back evidence of God in the soul while remaining true to our empirical foundations. This in an age of spiritual collapse without a parallel in human history.

    Mystagogues we have enough — some of them very eminent and amiable people. But their credentials are always suspect. Nobody really believes what they say, because they lack a scientific founda tion, and the Scientist is the Medicine Man of the modern age. In the old days, an evil generation sought after a sign: now, they ask for statistical confirmation!

Arthur Koestler's latest book, just published, *The Lotus and the Robot,* is a brilliant and caustic firsthand indictment based on personal encounters in the East with Hindu saints, yogis and Zen Buddhist adepts. He has struck a very great blow against the fashionable purveyors of oriental spirituality. Everyone is now saying that oriental mysticism has been exposed or exploded. Of course, the matter is not quite so simple as that. But my point is that this only underlines the lonely eminence of your own position.

The School of Analytical Psychology contains a number of brilliant names. [Here I mentioned three known to me in England.] But where is there anyone who combines the roles of Discoverer, Healer, Teacher and Artist?

. . . .

All this has to be taken against the background of the unexampled spiritual darkness of our time. I have lived for forty six years in England, and for the first time in my life I am really frightened — frightened, I mean, by the state of values in this country.

Why am I telling you all this? Because I want you to know the *immeasurable loss* it would be if you were to depart from among us. You are the living embodiment of your theories — not a half-man who had ascended by denying his body. The world would not be the same without you.

It is true, we all have to die. But my own instinct tells me that your life is not over; and I am filled with horror and indignation at the thought that your end might be hastened by the bigotry and persecution of narrow little minds. Of course, you cannot "fight your battles" at your age in the way you could twenty or thirty years ago. But what shocks me to the core is that you should be asked to do so. Where is the respect and consideration which are due to old age, even when old age has no other merit than itself to recommend it?

Up to this point, I had been trying to express my sympathy for Jung. But now I switched "to a more pragmatic level," and attempted to show why his ideas were not more widely appreciated and how the position was changing in his favour. This might appear to be the most awful goddam cheek; so I began by saying, "I am very conscious that my knowledge is extremely limited here, and that most of what I say will be familiar to you already." I also admitted that my experience was confined to England. Then I continued:

> Up to the end of the Second World War, though your name was well-known as one of the "Big Three," very little was known of your individual work. Now [here I quoted a friend of mine who is a W.E.A. extension lecturer], there is a "very general interest." This is attributed to two main factors—your television appearance and the issue of your *Collected Works*.
>
> Of course, your own researches into individuation date back many years now. But one must remember that *The Integration of the Personality* only appeared in English in 1940; and some of the large works of your later period have only recently become available.
>
> I suppose Freud's works began to appear in England in c. 1915. I know that the late Dr. William Brown claimed to be the first person to use the concept of the super-ego in England. That would have been in the early 1920s. The great wave and craze for Freudian psychoanalysis made its full impact in England only in the 1930s. Thus even if we date Freud's original discoveries to c. 1905 and not to the *Traumdeutung* of 1895, * there was a time-lag of between 25-35 years before they made their impact in England.
>
> I think it was Harold Laski who said that in England 16½ years had to elapse between the inception of an idea and its execution.
>
> In the case of anything so foreign to the natural bent of the English temperament as a psychological theory, a considerably longer period would have to be allowed!
>
> In a sense, Freud's ideas had an easier passage. They only had to break down the old-fashioned religious and conventional resistance. This was in line with the movement of the time. They swam along excellently with the revolutionary ferment of the thirties, when half the intelligentsia was hovering on the brink of "liberal" Communism, and anything subversive of the old order was highly acceptable to intellectual opinion. There was no psychological opposition to Freud's ideas, since at that time psychology was virtually unknown in this country.
>
> Thus it came about that a whole intellectual generation was "brought up" on Freud, as it were. And it is this generation who

---

*Freud's *Traumdeutung (Interpretation of Dreams)* was in fact first published in 1900.

now sit in newspaper offices and write reviews, etc. etc. etc. Of course,
once one has adopted a given system of ideas, it is a terrible wrench
to unpin them all again, rethink them and modify them in a new
direction. Take my own case. I suppose I may say I am an *anima
naturaliter Jungiana*** and therefore naturally receptive to your ideas!
But what happened to me? I had a big neurosis and very little money.
So I went to the Tavistock Clinic and had a moderate Freudian analysis (1939-c.1941). Up to a point, this was very good for me. It literally taught me the facts of life, and the importance of the first five
years and of the unconscious, and helped to break down some of
my crippling shyness. On the other hand, it "taught" me that history, Catholicism, the country—everything I was most passionately
interested in—were regressive products of my mother fixation. Thus
in a way it undermined my life. And it made me strive to become
a "normal" young man—strong, hearty, and knowing about timeta-
bles, etc.

I well remember the intense resistance I had to the idea of "archetypes" when Dr. Laudenheimer first raised the subject. I still had
this resistance years later, and it was only when I had an archetypal
dream myself—when an archetype kicked me in the solar plexus,
as it were—that I was forced involuntarily to think of your theories.

What has happened in general? Some of Freud's ideas and discoveries have passed into the general currency of educated
knowledge—and rightly so, for they were true as far as they went.
But the golden and roseate hopes of that first dawn period, when
it was really *believed* that in psychoanalysis was contained the mystic
key to the understanding and revealing of *everything*—these have
long since faded into gray nothing, and been replaced by a reaction
(typically British!) against psychology in general.

What are we left with today? Today we are living in an entirely
new period. The "social revolution" has come. The welfare state has
laid a foundation which assures the physical basis of life. Poverty,
malnutrition and mass unemployment have been abolished in their
grosser from. There are no longer any monstrous evils in this dimension to crusade against. Our evils are of a spiritual order—
materialism, irresponsibility and total moral and spiritual vacuity.

Socialist propaganda has been misunderstood to mean that as
all our social evils are caused by the wicked capitalist system, there
is nothing we can do about it. We cannot be expected to be grown-
up or responsible, etc, etc, etc. This is a distinct element, I believe,

*A soul naturally Jungian. See below, p. 176

in the psychology of the "Teddy-boy," the juvenile delinquent, and the "mixed-up kid." "We are just mixed-up kids. It is the job of society to love and understand us. It is not our job to do anything for society!"

In the sphere of religion, the situation is ghastly. It would be comic if it was not tragic. We are still supposed to be a Christian nation. Yet organised Christianity only touches 15% of our people *or less*. Very many people are living now in the second or third generation of agnostics. The remnants and relics of Christian morality which still served to hold life together for their parents are seen through as hollow shams and hypocrisy by the children. I am horrified to find that a number of young people take an actual pride in crimes of violence. This is a measure of our failure to pass on to them any kind of valid spiritual heritage.

And so there is this really vast and desperate problem — literally millions of people consciously or unconsciously hungering after some kind of spiritual guidance for their lives. Even if they are not conscious of any need, one can see it in their harassed, unfulfilled faces as they walk along the street.

Professor Jung, it is to meet *this* situation that *your* ideas are overwhelmingly needed. The negative process of the stripping down, the destruction and the demolition of our great European cultural heritage has been carried so far that it has developed an independent dynamism of its own and become one of our major industries! Human souls are being crushed in the process. What is needed is some *positive* technique for relating oneself to the totality of life and in so doing of discovering its meaning. Your psychology contains what is needed.

The failure — it is not really your failure at all — is a failure to confront the task of popularisation and publicity...

You yourself have given a very fine lead in your television interview. This is the medium that reaches people in their homes Even the educated world discovered — to its surprise! — that you are still alive!

My book is also an attempt to reach a rather wider audience...

But there is a great need for explanations that are simpler and more popular than this. I always think that anything great can be expressed in words of one syllable. I shall never forget Dr. Winifred Rushforth's report on how this was done at the Davidson Clinic. The four functions became the "four H's" — "Head, Heart, Hand, and Hunch"!

I think that introverted people have a tendency to shrink from advertisement. Admirable though this may be from one point of view, the fact remains that to do anything in the modern world it is necessary to accept the uses of publicity and to endure the discomforts involved. The main analysts in this country are too much involved with their patients to do very much writing, etc. But there ought to be somebody who can take up challenges as they come along. For instance, now that *Lady Chatterley's Lover* has been printed in the full, unexpurgated form, D.H. Lawrence is the most famous writer in England. Recently there was a talk printed in *The Listener* on D. H. Lawrence and Freud ('Two Honest Men' — Philip Rieff on Freud and D. H. Lawrence, *The Listener* May 5, 1960). Your name was not mentioned. Yet this writer *screams* for a Jungian interpretation. There are passages in *The Plumed Serpent* dealing with the old Mexican gods which might have been excerpts from your writings. Yet I do not think Lawrence knew your later work. I myself have neither the time nor the knowledge to write a book on this subject — but such a book certainly ought to be written.

I went on to report one hopeful experiment — P. W. Martin's article on "God, Sex and Society" in the February, 1959 issue of *Education for Teaching,* the journal of the Teachers' Training Colleges in England. "In it," I went on, "he deplored...the absence of the great initiation themes from the education of young people in England. The teachers are faced with the ghastly problem of giving guidance to children on questions of values when there are no values either in the children's homes or in the society into which they will go out to work.

"The article aroused enormous interest — it evidently touched some very live nerves. It was followed...by a brisk correspondence and also by a Symposium...on...'Religion and the Education of Teachers.' There is no doubt that your ideas were the positive inspiration behind this movement. What particularly surprised me was the virtual absence of hostile criticism.... The day is gone by when values could be inculcated in children by way of authority. Everything is questioned nowadays. Yet to transmit a vacuum would be treason indeed. Therefore, any ideas or any technique which make it possible to enter into a relationship with the creative spring inside each one of us come absolutely as a godsend..."

I sent on to consider the case of people who were "constitutionally incapable" of understanding Jung. These, I thought, were covered quite adequately by his own theory of psychological types. I continued:

> But there are others who are incapable because of avenues of mental perception are blocked by preconceived ideas. Orthodox Christians find it particularly difficult to make room for a psychological interpretation of their doctrines. This is not really so surprising. It is like a man in love whose mind is filled with the overwhelming image of his beloved. Then he hears this beloved praised and criticised for a totally different set of virtues and attractions, some of which seem contradictory to those he sees himself. His imagination is so preoccupied by his picture-image of the beloved that he simply cannot make room for somebody else's alternative estimate...

Finally, I switched back to the personal level.

> Please forgive this very long letter. Your letter aroused very strong feelings in me. I'm afraid I haven't devoted much time as yet to analysing these feelings psychologically! I happen to believe that there are certain situations where one just has to act on one's primary instincts. If psychology inhibits one from doing that, so much the worse for psychology!
>
> You have enriched my life so abundantly and so deeply over the course of the past fourteen years that I should be a traitor indeed if I withheld from you my reaction to the confidence you have reposed in me.
>
> Professor Jung, your letter has filled me with an overwhelming desire to meet you personally. It is true, I have wanted to see you before. However, up to now I have been too diffident to suggest it, and in any case, I do not think it would have been appropriate. Now, however, your letter has given me the courage to ask.
>
> . . . .
> At any time in December or subsequently, I could obtain leave...and come and see you at Zürich. If this idea is not con-

venient for you, please do not hesitate to let me know. I hate the idea of bothering you in any way. In any case, I must warn you that I am not in any way impressive. I am just another of those rather nervous people of whom you have probably seen far too many!

You have helped so many of these people. You have helped me too, enormously. Your psychology opens the way to those healing forces which are so desperately needed in the world today.

Thank you — and God bless you for all you have given us!

Yours sincerely,
Eugene Rolfe

By writing that tragic letter to me (a letter which could only have been written by a great man), Jung had given me the opportunity of a lifetime — a unique, priceless, unrepeatable pearl — to tell him exactly what I thought and felt about him — to speak to him as a lover speaks to his beloved.

The labourer is worthy of his hire, we are told. Like many others, Jung never received his wages. It was given into my hands to try to express our gratitude — to try to make good some tiny proportion of the years of neglect and vilification which were his recompense for standing to the truth as he saw it. Thank God I had the chance! And thank God I took it!

Soon after this letter went off to him, another letter from him to me arrived. The two missives had actually crossed in the post. Jung's letter read as follows:

19 Nov. 1960

Dear Sir,

Having finishing reading your book from cover to cover I am now better prepared, to give you my impressions or rather some of them. The theme itself is so rich, that one cannot hope to exhaust it. I have discovered quite a number of old friends in your book and I admire your wisdom and caution not to connect them with my name of ill omen. I can say: you have fulfilled your task to demonstrate the approach to Christianity to a christian-minded Agnostic. But if the latter should not be "christian-minded," but thoroughly blackened by the fires of Hell, which have broken through in Europe since 20 years now? — What then? It is beautiful to hear of the

Love of God again, but what about the Fear of God, the ominous message of the Evangelium Aeternum? πόθεν τὸ Κακόν? with one word. The Agnostics of our days are by no means all christian-minded. There is a terror, which goes much deeper. You call up again Tertullian's christian Anima of the first Roman centuries, which claimed the light, that shineth into the darkness. What about the Anima of our own benightet [sic] days? Let us hope that your readers will find their way back to the path of the centuries, the beautiful and spirit-filled baptisteria with their mystery, the Eucharist and its first emotions, the παντοκρατόρες ruling the spiritual universe. But there the ominous History of the World will begin again with the fearful question of the unredeemed darkness which comprehendeth not. The Sophisma of the *privatio boni* is too obviously thin.

By the way you seek the enigmatic oracle "Vocatus atque non vocatus deus aderit" in vain in Delphi: it is cut in stone over the door of my house in Küsnacht near Zürich and otherwise found in Erasmi collection of Adagia (XVIth Cen. Ed). It is a Delphic oracle though. It says: Yes, the god will be on the spot, but in what form and to what purpose? I have put the inscription there to remind my patients and myself: *Timor dei initium sapientiae.* Here another not less important road begins, not the approach to "Christianity" but to God himself and this seems to be the ultimate question.

Sincerely yours,
C. G. Jung

One or two references in this letter seem to call for an explanatory note. The *"Evangelium Aeternum"* ("Everlasting Gospel") comes from the Latin Vulgate version of Revelation XIV, 6, 7. In the English Authorised version, this passage reads:

"And I saw another angel fly in the midst of heaven, having the everlasting gospel to preach unto them that dwell on the earth, and to every nation, and kindred, and tongue, and people,

"Saying with a loud voice, *Fear God,* and give glory to him; for the hour of his judgement is come: and worship him that made heaven and earth, and the sea, and the fountains of waters" (the italics are mine). πόθεν τὸ Κακόν? ("pothen to kakon?" = "whence cometh evil?") links up with this same "ominous mes sage" about the "Fear of God" and the "terror, which goes much deeper."

Jung disagreed in principle with the classic formula of Christian theology; *Omne bonum a Deo: omne malum ab homine* ("All good comes from God: all evil from man"). This, he thought, laid far too heavy a burden of guilt on man's shoulders, and was in any case entirely one-sided. Jung's own view is nearer to the ancient Hebrew conception, according to which God caused evil as well as good, and created darkness as well as light.* His real criticism of Christianity was that by refusing to accept the dark side of God, it presented what was essentially a bowdlerised version of reality.

That is why he attacks "the sophism of the *privatio boni.*" The *privatio boni* is the Catholic doctrine that evil is essentially a "privation of good" and not, so to speak, a positive force in its own right. Jung would never accept any formulation which ran counter to his own psychological experience. This experience had led him to believe that good and evil, though relative to each other, are real opposites in the human psyche; and he stoutly resisted any form of mental jugglery (as he saw it) which tended to minimise the reality of evil. He had experienced evil in himself and in his patients; and he hadn't lived through the Hitler epoch for nothing. It is necessary for us mortals to come to terms with the whole range of reality, as it is, in its horror and its tragedy, as well as in its sweetness, in its savagery as well as in its divine love. Jung saw God as totality, not as perfection.

It is perfectly logical to entertain the opposite emotions of fear and love towards the same, one, inclusive object. Love embraces the whole world and unites me with all things: fear prevents me from getting run over in the street. The first merges me with the whole: the second secures my separate existence.

It is perfectly possible to ignore God. It does not follow that God can be ignored with impunity. "Called or not called, God

---

*"I form the light and create darkness: I make peace, and create evil: I the Lord do all these things." Isaiah 45:7

will be there." If we do call on him, he may appear as the source of all goodness. If we don't, he may visit us in a variety of scourges — as anything between a psychosomatic symptom and the explosion of a hydrogen bomb. It is in a wholesome terror of extermination that man's relationship with God begins. *Timor dei initium sapientiae;* the fear of God is the beginning of wisdom.

Παντοκρατόρες ("pantocratores" = "all rulers") must refer back to the discussion of the meaning of the word παντοκράτωρ ("pantocrator" = "all-ruler," wrongly translated as *omnipotens* in the Latin version of the Nicene Creed) on pp. 25-26 of my *Intelligent Agnostic,* where I had argued, following Prof. Geddes Mac-Gregor, that omnipotence does not necessarily belong to the idea of God in the Bible and the Creed. By putting it in the plural, Jung gives the word what seems like a Gnostic twist. The Gnostics lived in an archetypal world of ascending and descending hierarchies of spirits, ranged in tiers, rather like the seating in a theatre. The "all-rulers" of light in the spiritual universe would be contrasted, Jung plainly implies, with their opposite numbers in the realm of darkness. The gods are at one end, the pit at the other.

In *The Intelligent Agnostic's Introduction to Christianity,* I had stated that "Called or not called, God will be there" was the inscription over the door of the Delphic Oracle. I thought I had read this in an article about Jung. Jung now points out my mistake, gives the source of this aphorism, and tells me that it was cut in stone above the door of his own house at Küsnacht, Zürich.

Jung's two letters about my book are an excellent example of the bipolarity of the psyche. The first shows the light side of praise; the second, the darker side of criticism. The first is carried mainly by feeling; the second by thinking. Each, in its way, seems to me to be justified.

Jung hit the nail on the head when he said that my book was an introduction to Christianity intended for the "Christian-minded" agnostic. That was precisely the kind of reader I had, in point of fact, been writing for — though I hadn't articulated the thought so clearly. And Jung was kind enough to say that I had succeeded in this objective.

But his real criticism, like the terror, went much deeper. I myself had left out the Satanic aspect of reality, and its appropriate correlative on the part of man, an attitude of holy—or unholy—dread. The very distortion he'd criticised in Christianity had cropped up again in my *Intelligent Agnostic.*

This was off, because, of course, I was well aware of Jung's notions about the dark side of God, and had in fact included in my argument the following, most explicit statement:*

> We are the inheritors of a tradition that has split the devil clean off from God, forgetting that he was one of God's sons in the beginning, and that one of his titles is the bearer of light. And so we are left with the all-righteous monstrosity, a towering Father of unrelieved whiteness... All that is animal and lusty about man, together with the scheming adventurousness of his intelligence, is branded with the stigma of rebellion against the Most High and thrust down into hell (repressed into the unconscious), there to lower and lie in wait in a shape of black horror, as the Devil. We then get a completely distorted picture of life in terms of moral black and white, such as the worst type of parents used to impose on their children.

I had in fact reinterpreted God in terms of totality in the first half of the book, and then (so I imagined) applied this interpretation to the Eucharist in the second. But I had reckoned without my host.

Unlike Jung, who had approached the Mass objectively, from the outside, I was inside the tradition (if not inside the community); and I was interpreting the sacrament from the inside. I was still very much under the spell of the Eucharist, and I'd ended my book with the text of the rite in all its naked, uninterpreted simplicity. Unconsciously, I myself was still a prisoner of the con-

---

*The Intelligent Agnostic's Introduction to Christianity, p. 28 (hardcover edition).

cepts and the ethos interwoven with the words. The only darkness that appeared was in man's sin; on God's side, everything
was sweetness and light.

This accounts for the definite contrast in atmosphere between
the sturdy, earth-based independence of the first part of the book
(derived from Jung) and the tainted air of morbid guilt (derived
from the Christian communion service) which I couldn't help
scenting in the Eucharistic chapters. It accounts, too, for the
change in attitude between Jung's first and second letters about
my book.

Naturally, I was a bit disappointed by (though not at all *with*)
this letter. I had to surrender any hopes I may have cherished that
Jung would stamp my section on "Worship" with the cachet of
his approval as the authorized application of his ideas to the Anglican version of the Holy Eucharist. I was still convinced that
my interpretation contained a great deal that was valid, as far as
it went, but I had to admit that Jung's criticisms were justified
and that the whole idea of revamping Christianity left a large part
of the contemporary audience unstirred.

Rather more than two weeks went by after this, and then once
more post arrived from Switzerland. It was, in fact, the last letter I was ever to receive from Dr. C.G. Jung of Zürich. It was
type-written, and it occupied most of one side of one large, thin
sheet. Here it is:

    Prof. Dr. C.G. Jung   Küsnacht Zürich
                                               Seestrasse 228
                                          December 7, 1960

    Mr. Eugene Rolfe,
    44, Brampton Road,
    St. Albans.

Dear Mr. Rolfe,
Thank you for your long letter of November 21st. I see from it how
much you are shocked by the spiritual vacuum of our time. In this

respect you are indeed a kindred soul. When I complain about the
lack of echo, I don't mean publicity of which I got more than
enough, but rather the sad fact that there is almost no responce
(sic) from men aware of the appalling state of spiritual impoverish-
ment. Where are the *men* of our days? The few, who answered to
my call die early or get inflations by funking the issues.

H. D. Lawrence (sic) must have known of me through Mrs. . . . ,
his American ladyfriend who has married a Pueblo and had a house
in Taos, where he has lived for a while. His name was Antonio
Mirabal (or his brother's name?). I know him, but I cannot recall
her name in the moment (one of the plagues of old age!). She was
certainly acquainted with my ideas.

. . . .

Your Biblical analogies are perfectly legitimate, as they are archetypic experiences, which are repeated again and again, whenever a new idea is born, or when a hero-child appears in the world.
Time and again a light tries to pierce the darkness. Its bearer will
pay for it "dans ce meilleur des mondes possibles," as Candide says.
God himself must find it exceedingly difficult to get out from under the weight of his own creation. To live an archetypic life is no
reason for an inflation as it is the ordinary life of man. I have been
naiv (sic) in not expecting the darkness to be so dense.

If you can come out to Switzerland any time between now and
Xmas you are welcome on one of the following days: December
11th, 13th, 15th, 16th, 18th, 21st, preferably at 11 o'clock in the morning or than (sic) at 5 p.m. It will be practical for you to go to the
Hotel Sonne in Küsnacht and to send a cable to me as soon as
possible.

In the meantime, I remain, dear Sir,
            Yours sincerely,
            C. G. Jung.

This letter gave me some of the most blessed moments of pure,
unadulterated, golden happiness I have ever experienced in my
life. I was way up, high among the dizzy stars for quite a while —
perhaps even as long as half a day.

But at the same time, I had to go into action at once. My "Yes!"
to Jung's invitation was, of course, never in question. The only
points that remained outstanding were, simply, how and when.

In the first place, I decided to go overland, not fly, so that it would be a proper, regular, traditional journey; I remembered what Jung had once said about politicians who fly to international conferences: "Actually, they're not there at all—they're back home in their countries of origin."* I also decided to take three days' leave, so that the essential point of meeting would be islanded out, with a free day's space on either side.

I worked out that Friday 16th December would be the most convenient day for me and despatched a telegram to Jung, informing him of the date and the hour (11 o'clock).

Naturally, this precipitate plunge into the unfamiliar dimension of executive action had riveted my attention upon the last paragraph of Jung's letter. Thoughts about the rest of it arrived more slowly—some of them quite a long time afterwards.

I was delighted by Jung's expression, "In this respect you are indeed a kindred soul." It was not merely that the compliment was sweet and unalloyed. It seemed to me so generous and warmhearted of him. I was only too well aware of the yawning gulf between us. He was referring, of course, to the phrase *anima naturaliter Jungiana* ("a soul naturally Jungian") which I'd applied to myself in the letter he was replying to.

This in turn was a play on Tertullian's famous *anima naturaliter Christiana* ("the soul is naturally Christian"). I'd originally thought up this quip as a description of D. H. Lawrence, and it fits him a good deal better than myself.

It was news to me that D. H. Lawrence had had direct contact with Jung's later ideas. It was not until the following year, when I read Harry Moore's superbly comprehensive biography of Lawrence† that I was able to identify the "American ladyfriend." It was obviously the redoubtable Mrs. Mabel Dodge Luhan, Lawrence's original hostess in Taos.‡ In the light of this letter,

---

*Quoted   from   Memory.

†*The Intelligent Heart* (Penguin Edition, London, 1960)

‡She was at that time married to Mr. Antonio Luhan, a Pueblo Indian. In reality, Mabel does not seem to have been quite the unmitigated culture-vulture of Moore's decidedly one-sided account. See *The Improper Bohemians,* by Allen Churchill.

the possibility that Jung's ideas had some direct influence on Lawrence at the time when he was writing *The Plumed Serpent* cannot be excluded. This partially, but not wholly, invalidates my thesis that Lawrence was a naive paradigm of Jungian psychology.*

When he talks about men who "die early," Jung must certainly have had in his mind the tragic case of Erich Neumann, who had died in Tel Aviv the previous month (November, 1960). He was only 55 years old, but was carried away prematurely by cancer. Neumann (author of *The Origins and History of Consciousness, The Great Mother, Amor and Psyche* and of a brilliant and absolutely indispensable analysis of the sculptures of Henry Moore) was the only man in analytical psychology who might truly be said to have approached Jung himself in stature. Jung must certainly have looked to him to take a leading hand in carrying his work a generation further. His death, before Jung's own, must have been a correspondingly bitter blow. Other male colleagues who predeceased Jung were Richard Wilhelm, the sinologist (co-author with Jung of *The Secret of the Golden Flower*), and Dr. H. G. Baynes, who was Jung's principal representative in England from the twenties till the middle of the Second World War.

I must say, Jung's acceptance of my Scriptural parallels did relieve me quite a bit. I'd been worried about comparing Jung with Christ — even though it was clear enough from my letter that I was thinking about Christ as the tragic human bearer of light and not as himself a divine figure.

In his reply, Jung says that "to live an archetypic life is no reason for an inflation as it is the ordinary life of Man." This seems to me to point towards the essential distinction. All of us have access to the divine — or devilish — spark inside us, the heroic or the daemonic dimension — to "that of God" in every man, as

---

* Jung himself was in Arizona and New Mexico studying the Pueblo Indians in 1924-25. *The Plumed Serpent* was written in Mexico during 1923-25. But the two men never actually met. Lawrence's remarks about Jung in *Lorenzo in Taos* (Mabel's book about Lawrence) certainly do not suggest that he had imbibed Jung's ideas very deeply!

George Fox described it. Some such contact is actually the normal thing; without it, life is numb and sterilised. But this doesn't mean that we are obliged to *identify* our conscious ego with the treasure, so that it becomes our own, egotistical possession, as if a conjuror could produce God like a rabbit out of a hat.

Jung mentions the "archetypic experiences" which are "repeated again and again, whenever a new idea is born or when a hero-child appears in the world," and he goes on to say, "Time and again a light tries to piece the darkness. Its bearer will pay for it 'dans ce meilleur des mondes possibles.'" There is a differentiation here between "light" and its "bearer"; on the other hand, Jung speaks of a "hero-child" in a way that could certainly apply to himself.

Great men are *ex hypothesi* exceptional and in fact embody far more of the heroic than is allotted to us ordinary mortals. And the ego of a great man often possesses a strength corresponding to his mission in life — otherwise he would lack the sheer cussedness to carry through the programme required of him by his genius. I always think of Winston Churchill as an extravert counterpart of Jung in this respect. For all such men, the temptation to self-identification with the hero-archetype must be peculiarly insidious and devilish, since they are, in fact, heroic figures.

I wouldn't like to say myself that Jung never fell into this particular trap. The fact that he was so widely and unjustly rejected would make the temptation even more compelling. But if humour and modesty and the power to make human contact can be taken as the outward and visible sign of the inward and spiritual grace of non-identification, then we can be quite sure that, by and large, Jung retained his sanity. The very concept of "inflation" is a witness to his insight.

But these are later reflections. To continue with the effect the letter had on me at the time: I was not so much inflated as hyperbolically *elated* — "high," as they now call it — right high up in the sky. It was really a kind of erotic fulfillment — a sort of blessed success and acceptance in love.

XI

XII

XIII

XIV

XXX
Preparation _____

ext morning (10th December, 1960), I had the following dream:

    I was swimming over places where there was either insufficient depth of water, or else the stretches of water were divided by breakwater things or bars which impeded free, flowing movement. Finally I reached some higher ground, and from there I could look down and see, at a still lower level, left to right, a long expanse or lake of water which seemed to offer possibilities of free swimming. I noticed that my boots or shoes were soaking, and was somewhat surprised to think I had apparently been trying to swim fully clothed!

    I then must have found my coat hanging up or over the back of a bench; and I was horrified to find that all my money—everything I had taken out for the journey—was stolen, and replaced by a blue shiny case (rather like a lightish bluebottle in colour). All my wallets, etc, were gone.

This dream pulled me up short with a terrible jolt. Apparently, in my elation, I was plunging into water fully dressed, in a completely reckless and irresponsible manner: as a result, I had lost the money for the journey.

I interpreted the dream as a sharp warning that I was rushing into the crucial encounter with Jung in a slapdash, quite superficial spirit, without any attempt at serious preparation. From that moment, I started to look in and to prepare myself more steadily to meet the future.

Three days later, on the 13th December (*i.e.*, halfway between the first dream and the date of my appointment to meet Jung), I had a second dream. It went as follows:

> I seemed to be at some Evangelical meeting, possibly at a church hall. After some time, as nothing happened, I got up and left — apparently to go to bed. (This part of the dream was very vague. The second episode was very clear).
>
> Dr. Jung was sitting on a bench outside his house. He was white-haired, old, and extremely friendly, and he told me his mother had just died.
>
> I was acutely surprised, and said, "She must be very old!"
>
> "Oh! I just found her in bed upstairs!" he said, in an exceedingly calm, almost offhand manner, at the same time waving his hand to indicate the rear portion of the house.

It's reasonable to suppose that this dream represents the first fruits of my resolve to practise introversion, the whole situation being obviously dominated by the imminent prospect of my encounter with Jung.

My old passion for Catholicism (Anglican and Roman) had been loosening its grip a bit lately. There is an Evangelical Church round the corner from where we live, and my daughter belonged to a youth group there, though I never attended this church myself. So I may have had a vague feeling that there might be something to be said for religion of this kind. After all, Jung himself was an unrepentant Protestant, and it was the faith in which my own mother had been mainly educated.

In the dream, I try it out and find there's nothing doing in this direction. To me, it means a form of conventional religion I just have to leave behind;* so I simply get up and walk out. Going home to bed could mean turning in to meditate; perhaps then an individual solution might be found.

Really, my overwhelming interest is in the person of Jung himself; and, sure enough, in the second episode of the dream, Jung does himself appear in person. He may be the bearer of the *lysis,* or solution.

In my conscious mind I had been painting a picture of Jung as of a rather severe old fellow, with his agnostics "blackened by the fires of Hell," his "terror that goes far deeper" and his talk about the "Fear of God." Also, the photo of him in *The Listener* which accompanied Frieda Fordham's explanatory article about the TV appearance did show him as a potent old prophet indeed—rather formidable, somehow.

By contrast, the dream now comes up with a completely benign, white-haired old man, sitting, like Caspar, outside his door in the sun. His friendliness to me may be partly, in fact, a reflection of my own more positive approach to the unconscious.

I'm just about to visit Jung, and we may suppose that the dream may have something to say about what this great event *means* to me. But it wasn't until I called to mind a much earlier dream about a visit to Jung that the meaning began to glimmer through more clearly.

Some years ago, a long while before an actual *rencontre* had crossed the horizon of practical possibilities, but at a time when my *thoughts* were all the same very much turned in Jung's direction, I dreamed that I was actually visiting Jung in Zürich.†

I was admitted into the hall passage of a very narrow, apparently lower-middle-class villa, and there was Jung, on the left in-

---

*This is a personal statement. I would not dream of denying that Evangelical Christianity is still a valid faith for millions of people.
†The date of the dream was 22nd March 1954. In the text, I have printed my recollections of this dream.

side the door. His face looked large and round and moon-like, but the *back* of his head (very distinct — all the emphasis was laid on this) was the head of an awful slatternly woman, with dreadful matted hair in a ghastly mess.

I realised clearly enough when I thought about this dream that the female side of myself must have been in horrible disorder. The clear round face, in which all was clarity and light, was not very much more than a facade covering my tangled problems. The *personality,* concentrated in the head, though partly affected by a clear and limpid Jungian integration, was mostly fixed in the horrible clutch of this kind of negative Gorgon-Mother. It was an impersonal, not a personal, mother-figure.

On the other hand, the fact that I was actually visiting Jung in this dream and that the situation was at least clearly constellated seems to indicate that the journey of integration was under way, and that the problem was in some sense being tackled.

The narrow, lower middle-class villa (the polar opposite of the real Jung's surroundings) no doubt symbolised my fixation in the peculiar, dingy environment of those days. And this, in turn, was the outer shell attracted to itself by my continual involvement with the Gorgon-Mother.

In the *new* version, my Self (for that, I take it, is what Jung means to me) is right *outside* the house, sitting at ease in the open in the sunlight. He tells me quite casually that his mother is dead. She was *upstairs, inside* the house, and *in bed* — i.e., at two, or possibly three, levels' remove from outside reality. But the Self has at last emerged from its integuments, and is sitting outside, enjoying the sun. The calm, matter-of-fact tone (so inadequate as an expression of personal bereavement) in fact denotes acceptance and the settlement of the problem; the mother-fixation in its old from had simply been left behind — dead.

We must remember that this dream is the product of a relationship, not a champion weight-lifting achievement of my ego. It was Jung's "great" letter to me, my offer to visit him, his acceptance of my offer, my acceptance of his invitation, the first dream and the subsequent deliberate introversion — all this had precipitated a crisis in development. What Jung did smote right through to the heart, like a blow on the emotional solar-plexus. It stunned me — at least! — into opening my eyes, like a dope-ridden middle-aged Sleeping Beauty whole beauty consisted in the avoidance of masculine responsibilities and whose sleep had been protracted to the brink of the climacteric. It amounted to a supreme challenge to come right out of my safe little rabbit-hutch of routine and meet a great man face to face. I went over from the mother's to the father's camp, a step I'd failed to take at the age of three. But it took a Jung to make me take it!

All the same, we have to try to keep a sense of proportion. If I'd danced about and shouted "Hooray! I'm cured!" it would have been quite simply not true. I still had compulsive symptoms and was terribly undeveloped and infantile in many ways, particularly in some of my social relationships. The dream is an announcement of possibilities — a *prediction,* not of the E.S.P. kind, but in the sense of the statement of a trend. The personal me was nowhere near the Wise Old Man level — even though I was going "over there on a visit." And frankly, the kind, wise serenity of age was not yet quite my cup of tea. I could see it might be coming along, but I was a shade disappointed by the absence of vitality.

Another thing: I naturally wanted to keep this dream entirely for myself. It was so superbly, diaphanously transparent, and the cap seemed to fit me at every point. It scarcely even occurred to my mind that it might have some actual reference to *Jung* — that I might have to *share* the dream with him. My intuition told me that he wasn't dead yet, that he still had some life left in him. I didn't know that he would in fact die within six months of my visit to him.

But after the event I was compelled to reckon with the possibility that the dream might have foretold Jung's own demise (the Mother being the physical basis of life). It could have heralded the dissolution of my own mother-complex at the same time. There is nothing theoretically impossible about this — in fact, in some strange mysterious way, the two events may actually have been interconnected.

This would imply that the dream, in its reference to Jung at any rate, contained an element of straight E.S.P. prediction. I personally don't claim to know. And I'm not prepared to stick my neck out far enough in either direction to commit myself to a definite *pronunciamento!* But I should be dishonest if I failed to record the hypothesis. To my mind, it is exactly as unscientific to refuse to entertain a possibility of this kind as it is to bow down in blind credulity and humbly avow it must necessarily be so.

Before I finally took off for Zürich, I assembled a few inconsiderable items (publications), which I felt I'd like to present to Jung. To begin with, there were two numbers of *Corona,* of all things (it is "The Journal of Her Majesty's Overseas Service"). The first (from June, 1960) contained a delightful short memoir of Jung ("Dr. Jung, I presume," by F. D. Hislop), describing a chance meeting between Jung and a young Assistant District Commissioner off the beaten track in Kenya in 1925. The second (for December, 1960) contained a letter I'd contributed myself, supplying one or two additional facts about Jung's expedition to Mt. Elgon.

The there was an article on "The Significance of Psychotic Experience," by H. Osmond and J. Smythies, in *The Hibbert Journal* for April, 1959. Osmond and Smythies are two British psychiatrists, both working in North America, who are experienced in the field of hallucinogenic drugs such as mescaline and L.S.D. In the course of this important article they wrote: "We would urge that in order to understand schizophrenia it is necessary to grasp the reality of the existence of the Jungian collective unconscious — the *mundus archetypus* — as an autonomous realm of existence, greatly to be admired and feared and which we can examine most easily in the form of the sense-data observable under the influence of mescaline. It is the greatness of Jung to have recognised this fact."

Next came the English translation of Rudolf Otto's *The Idea of the Holy* in the Pelican edition (1959). I included this because of the translator's Appendix on "The Expression of the Numinous in English." I was quite sure this would interest Jung.

The final item was to have been D. H. Lawrence's *The Plumed Serpent,* but this was out of print at the time and I didn't succeed in tracking down a copy. What I bought instead was nothing less than the famous unexpurgated Penguin edition of *Lady Chatterley's Lover,* which had been a *cause célèbre* a few months earlier. The girl who served me with this book in a shop by the Odeon in Leicester square was an irresistibly attractive anima-figure, who made it, Jung, herself and even me seem appropriate associates in every respect!

XXXI
Encounter with Jung _____

I set off from Victoria in the early afternoon of 14th December, 1960, and travelled through the night, arriving at Zürich at breakfast time on the following morning. I spent a couple of hours in Zürich itself, where I felt entirely at home. I walked along the banks of the Limmat, and had a look at Zwingli's church, the Grossmünster, "the Mother Church of the Swiss German Reformation." Then I caught the local train to Küsnacht, which is fourteen kilometres southward from the town centre, along the eastern shore of the lake. I arrived there in the early afternoon.

At the Hotel Sonne, an unassuming, democratic young Swiss girl showed me into a bedroom on the first floor of the Annexe building directly overlooking the lake. By the window was a light, leanback armchair which one could turn arcwise to right or left so that different segments of the lake became visible. I undid my case and arranged my things. Then I sat down in the armchair and looked out over the lake.

I was terribly, overwhelmingly tired — tired right out beyond all measure — and I must have sat there for several hours. All the exhaustion of my life, which was full of an almost continuous exhaustion, seemed to come crowding upon me at once, on top of the ordinary tiredness after the train and the excitement of the adventure and the preparation.

But oh! the blessed relief of just sitting there and looking at the waves coming lapping in over the lake! Surely some god or divine power must have granted me this blessed space of pause and respite! I knew it was one of the moments of my life. It was like being on a retreat. In front of me was my meeting with Jung: behind me was the whole bitter littleness of my life, with all the anxiety and stress and hurry and the endless travelling and rushing about.

The water was entirely *natural* — it was like a lake in virgin country in Kenya. There was not a sign of industrialism in sight — just the clean, natural water — a light gray in colour. Every now and again the delightful little lake steamers — spotlessly white, riding buoyantly like swans — came chugging in the landing stage, which was directly behind the hotel, about twenty yards to the right of where I was sitting. Then they went teetering comfortably away, and were to be seen passing and repassing zig-zag in midlake, like slightly erratic water-trams.

It was the *water* which absorbed me in this Swiss scene. As I've said, it was an entirely natural element — the perfect counterpoise, in fact, to the artificialities of industrial life — an element in which you really could become absorbed, all cuts and clutches smoothed away, and emerge reborn and whole again. It was a natural symbol and a symbol of nature.

A return to the womb? Of course it was, but to the womb as the primary source of life. Escape from "reality"? Naturally, and why not? It was the same kind of escape from "reality" that you get from a holiday in the Lake District or a night's clear, untroubled sleep.

For myself, at that particular moment, I can only say from my heart, in all sincerity: the waves of Lake Zürich were the waters of healing. It was in these really wonderful and paradisal surround-ings that I tried to prepare myself for my "Encounter with Jung." I didn't bother much about the symbolism at the time. I just tried to pray (rather dumbly) that I might be made ready. Under the cooling and soothing influence of those waters I could be con-scious of *some* of my imperfect motives; and some of the impurities — *my* impurities — did seem to leave me.

It was quite well on in the afternoon before I finally did bestir myself. The Hotel Sonne is actually on the Seestrasse, but I wanted to reconnoitre the ground thoroughly and find out exactly where no. 228 was and how long it would take me to get there in the morning.

Almost the first thing that met my eyes as I sallied forth along the lake side of the street was a metal plate, announcing in large black letters, Dr. So-and-So's "NERVENKLINIK." I resisted a momentary inclination to identify this establishment with Dr. Jung. Then I thought, "Perhaps I'd better go in there myself for a short burst of treatment before I see the great man!"

I walked along for about ten minutes, past residential houses, with sort of country paths or wide tracks at intervals between them, leading down irregularly to the lake. Then suddenly I saw an unusually tall house, standing very upright well back from the road and at the bottom of a steep incline descending to the lake bank. I immediately thought, *"This* is something!" It certainly did give the impression of being the residence of somebody im-portant.

It was about two-and-a half stories high, the plaster was yellow-gold, and the windows had blue or bluey-green shutters (rather faded with age and indeterminate in colour). There was a steep-ish red tiled roof, and in front of the house was a circular turret tapering to a point, definitely in the medieval castellan style. There was no plate on the gate, or any indication of a number, but I was able to fix it beyond doubt. It was Jung's house, all right!

This house of Jung's fascinated me almost unbearably. For one thing, in style, period and class it had an unmistakable family connection with some of the houses in the "Saints" district in Bedford, where I was brought up — except that this was a far larger and more spacious conception. And it kindled the dormant fire of the romantic inside me. One could easily imagine the aged alchemist poring over his manuscripts and his instruments at dead of night in the windowed room under the roof of the turret!

I walked rather circumspectly by — I was quite morbidly anxious not to be seen, and not to be thought to be prying. A straight drive plunged down steeply from the gate to the front door — or rather, portal — over which a single brilliant naked light was burning, as if to emphasise the claim that the occupant of this rather old-fashioned house was still a force to be reckoned with in the contemporary situation. It really was extraordinary to think that Jung, the last surviving member of the historic triumvirate of depth psychology, was actually living here. Sigmund Freud had been entertained in that house.

I walked on. Next door to Jung's house was a brand new modern "Strandbad." A little further on, I came to a small church, with a slim, pointed spire, quite delicate, sheathed in bright pastel green. This had a clock by which I could tell the time.

I turned back. I was feeling really invigorated now after my long rest, and I thoroughly enjoyed the walk. I went down a track to the lakeside at a place where there was a bit of free shore, with a small park behind it. I stooped down and dipped my hands in the water. I was delighted to find it clean and clear — you could see the bottom and the rocks in it. No smirch, no stench, no stain — and this was in hardworking Switzerland, where Ruskin was already complaining of the pollution of the pure lakes by industrial processes a hundred years ago!

I was extremely pleased by Küsnacht. The whole place is evidently a residential suburb, built out round the nucleus of a small lakeside village. I suppose I shall always be one of those deplorable types to whom surroundings are more important than people. At all events, I hadn't fully realised until then how much I'd suffered from the years of exile in the industrial wilderness. I felt entirely at home and relaxed here.

I was filled with a sort of yearning sorrow and compassion for Jung, whom I thought of as old and lonely and disappointed — again, like my father, in a way — and very much like myself. All three of us came from the same academic background, and all three of us were somehow lonely, unrecognised figures.

That night, at the hotel, I dined alone. After the meal, I returned to my refuge and sat down again in the armchair by the window. The view at night over the lake was simply magical. The little landing stage for the steamerettes was flanked by two small lamp-posts, and there was a third on the near side. The lamps were bright yellow, red and green, and they were surmounted by odd little circular hats. They swayed in the wind like Chinese lanterns. The steamerettes still came teetering in and out, at intervals.

Across the lake, the houses had disappeared. Instead, I could see a long, fantastically beautiful coronal of lights which wreathed its way along the opposite shore. This was the view which Thomas Mann had admired so much in his last years. It looks for all the world like a terrestrial lakeside Milky Way — and this explains Jung's remark in "Flying Saucers," where in commenting on the Yves Tanguy picture he comes down personally in favour of the view that the long light strips are a shoreside city seen from above at night.*

Finally, I got everything ready for the morning, wrote a bit, went to bed, and slept excellently. On the day itself, I had a little time to spare; so I strolled inland among the houses and gardens of Küsnacht, which reminded me of Esslingen in Swabia: very pleasant, open and countrified in the German continental manner. Controlling my meander rather carefully, I soon came down to Seestrasse once again, and retraced my route of the previous evening. Rather earlier than I had expected, the tall, unmistakable form of Maison Jung hove into view. As I passed it, I noticed

*Jung, "Flying Saucers," *C.W.* I, plate IV.

a big round electric clock on a garage, directly opposite.

I determined I would carry on till ten to eleven, and I finally turned round in full sight of the clock on the slender church spire further on. I was getting a little excited by now. When I repassed the house, the garageclock informed me there were just two minutes to go. I walked on, but only a few paces further. I turned back, and found myself opposite Jung's gate.

At one minute to eleven I swung into the steep drive which sweeps down to Jung's front door. There was a big Mercedes-Benz car outside, and a chauffeur busied about it.

The door itself is double-breasted (if "double-portalled" isn't a better word!). It is also unusually lofty, and above it is the Delphic oracle inscribed in Latin capitals: VOCATVS ATQVE NON VOCATVS DEVS ADERIT.

Above that again was another Latin inscription. Before I had time to read it through, however, the front door was opened. A comfortable Englishwoman with whitish hair invited me in.

"Mr. Rolfe — or is it *Dr.* Rolfe?" she asked.

"Mr.," I replied. "I'm very much *lay!*"

As I said this, in a slightly bass, rotundo, stomachic voice, I felt a good old-fashioned middle-class assumption of grandness and essential rightness; I felt an assurance that I was all right and accepted, as it were — just as I imagine a detribalised African might feel on a return visit to his native kraal!

"And how did you leave England?," asked Miss Bailey (for it was obviously Miss Ruth Bailey, Jung's English house-keeper, who had let me in). She spoke in the manner of the voluntary expatriate, enquiring after her home country. I wasn't quite sure in what precise sense this enquiry was intended, but I said something about its having been very wet, and that it was only just beginning to work up to the cold appropriate to the season.

She took me up the broad steep staircase (we walked very comfortably side by side), and showed me into a small room leading off the landing at the right.

"You can put your coat here," she told me, indicating a

coathanger behind the door. "I'll tell the Professor—he won't be a moment."

I hung my coat up as requested, and placed down my gloves on a small round table in the centre. This was already occupied by a note-book and pencil, as if for recording appointments with a patient, and I confess I had a moment's compulsive anxiety about my gloves being too close to the notebook, which I suppose puts me firmly into the patient class. However, I got over this pretty quickly and left my gloves undisturbed instead of trying to put them into my coat pocket.

The little room was indescribably full of atmosphere—like a potpourri from our grandmother's days. There were faded wicker chairs with pinky-red plush seats, and a sofa of the same kind and period (on which I sat myself). There was a sort of neo-Louis XV elegance about the furniture.

On the wall to my right, which formed one end of this small oblong chamber, there was a print showing Castor and Pollux on horseback, with a woman falling down naked between them.* It was a central European print of the style popular (I should say) between about 1890 and 1914. Next to it hung a portrait of Schiller, showing his prominent questing nose and forehead and his indescribable air of aspiring idealism.

Behind me, next to the window on the opposite wall, I believe, was a smallish picture (some sort of a *Stich*) showing a naked man (very thin and Gothic), just startled out of bed and standing up, petrified with fright, beside it. To the left was a tall, spindle-legged, stork-like apparition in white, its spookish nature marked by its round human head. I failed to decipher the small, quasi-manuscript inscription underneath it. These pictures reminded me forcibly of Dr. Laudenheimer's room in Cambridge.

On the long wall opposite me, at the other end from the door, there was a column of bookshelves, tall, but not wide; it contained,

---

*At the time, I couldn't identify the woman. Later, I thought it was Helen of Troy. In fact it was almost certainly one of the daughters of Lycippus.

I noticed, among other things, a series of volumes on the "Cultural Heritage of India" (in English).

The carpet, which had rather more vivid colours, and patterns like those I remembered from my boyhood, may have dated from a slightly later period than some of the other accoutrements of the room. But the whole place was *redolent* of the initial psychoanalytical period—Central European, bourgeois, 1905-1914. It reminded me pungently (giving the smell) of the world that can be glimpsed through the pages of Freud's *Interpretations of Dreams.* One might almost have been one of the original patients, waiting for the resolution of a compulsion neurosis—a pattern into which (apart from the time-lag) I suppose I didn't fit altogether too badly. It was the period into which I had actually been born.

At last the door opened, and a little wisp of a woman with small, intent brown eyes came in and told me that Jung was ready to see me. She was the secretary, she explained. She took me round to the study.

The room into which she ushered me was quite unlike the one I'd left. It was a room that was lived in, not a period piece. It was a large, lofty, hall-like chamber, stately but comfortable, full of books and pictures and objects and furniture.

Jung himself—a tall, big, white-haired old man—was by the window and came over to meet me. There was practically only one thing I'd prepared beforehand to say to Jung—and that was an opening gambit. So I came out with it at once: "I'm so glad you said yes!" (This had seemed to me more appropriate than thanking him for an invitation, when the initiative had in fact come from my side).

"Well," he replied, "I was curious to see who it was who had such a concern." (He was referring to the spiritual vacuum we had been talking about in our letters).

The voice was high, humorous and ironic. You could say there was a smile with a twinkle in it. It was also high-powered and intellectually sophisticated. In a flash you felt you were in the presence of a firstclass mind, whose owner was also a man of the world. Here was someone out of the top drawer of international scholarship, yet somehow oddly English rather than Germanic in quality.* It was rather like talking to an Oxford don with the personality calibre of Winston Churchill.

Jung put me into a chair tête-á-tête with his own. *His* chair was directly against the window and commanded a view out over the lake. Both of these were comfortable armchairs—with straightish backs, however, so that you could sit at ease and yet alert and comfortably facing one another. There was no hint of the "Jesuit" technique practised by Aramis in *The Three Musketeers,* whereby the interlocutor sat shadowed and shrouded in darkness while the light fell full on the face of the "victim." Jung had the light full on his face—whereas I, though visible, was not illuminated. I had the quite distinct impression that Jung really did enjoy meeting people.

At the beginning of our talk, I brought out my presents: I put *Corona* for June 1960 on the edge of the small table on my right; here Jung laid down his pipe. He asked me if I wanted to smoke, and when I said I didn't, he asked me if I minded if he smoked himself. Of course, I said no; but I was touched by this little courtesy.

I told Jung that years ago (when I saw a photograph of him at my analyst's) I was relieved to find that he used *matches* to light his pipe. This gave me a feeling of familiarity—it was like my father.

"Yes. I don't go in for gadgets," he replied.

Sure enough, at that very moment I caught sight of a silver metal lighter, lying on the table by the side of his pipe.

"I'm old fashioned," Jung went on, humorously, "I come up gradually, by decades—I do use a lighter now!"

I confessed to Jung that I had never managed to type, and always wrote things out by pen.

---

*"The older Jung grew, the more English he looked." I'm indebted to the late Mr. Geoffrey Watkins for this perceptive comment.

"Oh, I leave typing to my secretary," he said.

I told him how much he reminded me of my father.

"What was your father?" Jung asked.

"A schoolmaster. He was a classical scholar like you, and came from the same sort of family. Of course, he was entirely unlike you in having no use of any inward life. All looking within was morbid, and talking about one's feelings was bad manners."

I told Jung that when I received his letter I had been so happy that I didn't know what to do.

"But then I had a dream which showed me the other side. I was trying to swim and there were difficulties in the water, and I discovered that my shoes were soaked and I must have been swimming with my clothes on. Also, I had lost all my money. So I thought I must have been plunging into this thing with no adequate preparation."

"Ah. You've been getting into deep water there, "Jung replied.

As we were talking, I looked a good deal at Jung, though it was rather a question of stealing glances (I shrank from the rudeness of a steady gaze). I had the impression of someone so extremely old that he was almost beyond recalling. The eyes were deep and rather sunken in their sockets, and the skin underneath them almost transparent. The hands, too, looked rather pale.

But as we talked and he gradually warmed to the subject that had been the passion of his whole long lifetime, the ancient fire leaped up inside him and there was a really wonderful play of the spirit. It inspired me, in fact, with an unusual reflection. It made me wonder what spirit is, that is can transcend the limitations of such an aged body.

The magnificent high broad lined forehead which is so prominent (*e.g.* in Douglas Glass's *Sunday Times* portrait) was there, all right, and unmistakable—yet the gentle, warm, healthy colouring of the face seemed to soften its severity and tensile strength. He looked relaxed and in repose. The nose was large, well-formed and not un-Jewish in appearance (a very cultivated Jewish man from Vienna that I made friends with on the journey home told

me it was in fact a *Swiss* nose!). But the most striking first impression of the face was undoubtedly the wonderfully sensitive
mouth, alive and most expressive of humour and feeling. I have
never seen such an expressive mouth on a man. There was nothing weak about it, but it made think me at one of Jung's own
celebrated concept of the anima. As always, Jung embodied his
own teaching. This was the famous female side of man!

The well-known white moustache was also there, of course; but
it was small and not obtrusive. It was not until later that I noticed the colour of Jung's eyes — a very fine, golden brown.

It was one of the most *living* faces I have ever seen, a face that
had constantly expressed thought and feeling and was the polar
opposite of that stolid and impassive mask by means of which
the crustier type of Englishman seeks to conceal his reactions (if
any!) from his contemporaries. *Montrer son visage naturel* is the
advice (Jung once said) the Buddhists give us. Jung certainly
showed his.

He was, of course, most decidedly a *big* man, with big legs inside the flannel trousers. He was wearing a lightish gray jacket
which gave some indication of the breadth of his shoulders. He
had a bright, reddish, woollen tie.

I felt no kind of embarrassment with Jung. But during the early
part of our talk I was anxious in another way. I was consumed
by the painful consciousness that here, in front of my very eyes,
was Jung — Jung himself in all his Jungness — that this was it, the
real thing, the actual meeting, and that in a terribly short time
it would all be over, gone for ever. So I was strained to catch it,
to hold it, not to lose it — the face in particular, but that really
only as the appearance of the personality. This feeling insensibly
wore off, as I — and perhaps he too — warmed up and a bond of
rapport was formed between us.

I told Jung that the copy of *Corona* on the table contained an
account of a meeting with him by an Assistant District Commissioner at Kapsabet in Kenya (I had sweated blood to memorise
this name!). There was a moment of blankness followed by al-

most instant recollection.

"Yes! I remember Mr. Hislop. There was a lot of trouble about passports and regulations, and I had to see him. I had lunch with him. I remember that his wife had some of my books and I was interested to find them right out there in Africa."

Jung told me he went to Africa "to study the primitive in myself." I was very much struck by this expression. Even at that date (in 1925), he was concerned with what the investigation meant internally.

"I wanted to find out what the Negro meant to me," Jung went on, "I studied my dreams, and the whole time I was in Africa I didn't once dream of a Negro. And then at last I did dream I was in a hairdressing saloon and a Negro dressed in a white coat cut my hair. But there seemed to be something familiar to me about his face. I thought, and at last I remembered: it was a Negro I knew from Kentucky."

"So you imported a Negro who had been subjected to our civilisation," I replied.

"No," Jung replied. "I came to the conclusion that I was defending myself against the Negro. That is always the danger — you see it in people who have lived long in the tropics." (Jung used this expression more than once).

"That they go native," I suggested, continuing his sentence.

"Yes, it gets them all in the end. The men hold out longer than the women — the men have their ideas and so on..."

"But the woman is nearer to the earth?" I suggested.

"Once in East Africa, at Dar-es-Salaam, I saw a row of tribal chiefs and noticed, to my astonishment, a white woman among them. She actually addressed me in excellent English. She had been the wife of a missionary, but it had got her, and she had married one of the tribal chiefs."

"D. H. Lawrence's American lady-friend married a Pueblo," I said, resuming the thread of Jung's last letter.

"Yes! I have stayed in her house in Taos, New Mexico," Jung replied. "I can't remember her name now. I could remember all these things a few years ago. That is my old age!"

I had been reading up Richard Aldington's Introduction to the Penguin edition of *The Plumed Serpent*. So now I came out with the information that *The Plumed Serpent* was written in 1923 and 1924 (my memory is bad, too, and I couldn't remember the actual months).*

"That is about the time," Jung said (Jung was actually in Arizona and New Mexico, studying the Pueblo Indians, in 1924-1925. I had looked this up for my *Corona* letter).

"And he deals with a white woman, Kate O'Brien, who marries a Pueblo Indian chief," I went on.

"Ah, that's it," Jung said.

I asked Jung whether Miss Bailey hadn't been concerned about the expedition he made to Mt. Elgon.

"Did you meet her — a blonde woman?," Jung asked me in reply.

"Yes," I said.

"She was entrusted," Jung continued, "to my charge by the Governor of Uganda, as she was to make the journey home via the Sudan, and it was quite impossible at that time for a woman to make such a journey alone, or just accompanied by 'boys.' Sudan was at that time under the Anglo-Egyptian Condominium."

"And that was the hour of destiny for her?" I asked (meaning that she threw in her lot with Jung!).

I'm not quite sure precisely what Jung thought about this expression, but like the ordinand and the Thirty-Nine Articles, he signified his agreement in a general sense.

"What sort of reviews did you get for your book?" Jung asked me.

I said I'd had nineteen, mostly fairly favourable, with the exception of about four or five, which were all from orthodox Christians, more or less-for understandable reasons.

"They were afraid," Jung said. "I remember Temple, when he

---

*More accurately, the period was from May 1923 to February 1925. See The *Intelligent Heart,* by Harry Moore, Penguin ed., pp.389, 415.

was Archbishop of York, inviting me to talking to a group of his clergy — clergy of his — I don't know what."

(This was the only time Jung hesitated for lack of an appropriate English word — pardonably enough, since what he was groping for was presumably the rather technical "Province" or "Archdiocese"). "And Temple admitted that the Church's doctrine of the Holy Spirit was inadequate. They were interested in Satan, and when they asked me about this, I replied: 'There is only one way of gaining knowledge of such a figure, and that is by way of direct experience.' And I offered Temple — I said, 'Send me one of your priests and I will take him and train him and show him about it — free of charge. And then he can come back and train his brother clergy' — Nothing! I heard nothing further from him. They were afraid. Quite simply, they were afraid.

"It was very bad, because Temple did see something — and when you see something like that and fail to draw the consequence it is like the sin against the Holy Ghost. He was a very good man, but too much a Prince of the Church — considerations of Church policy and worldly matters — it is very bad when such things come in."

"But at least he asked you," I said.

"That makes it worse," Jung replied.

I remembered Dr. Temple's disappointingly early death, just when such great things had been prophesied for him at Canterbury. And I also remembered that he used to carry a portable typewriter about with him on his travels, so that he could continue working on this correspondence even on the train.

"I have the impression that Dr. Temple drove himself rather hard," I said.

"He was driven," Jung replied, emphatically. This, coming out with the continental "r" and also *mit dem Brustton der Uberzeugung,** made a singularly impressive statement.

Jung told me that the Holy Spirit and the Trinity were contained in the (ancient) Egyptian religion. "There was a bull who

*With the deep voice of complete conviction.

was the father of his own mother. Oh yes, it was all there!"*

I must have been looking away slightly to the left — slightly toward the left side of the window, that is — and therefore, to that extent, away from Jung. I was not aware of not attending, but I was just that trifle visually distracted.

"I can tell you some more about this — if you are interested," Jung said. My wandering eyes returned at once.

"Of course!," I said immediately, and with emphasis. I was acutely penitent at having been asked.

"I have heard it said that the Egyptian religion had virtually no influence on Christianity. But the Egyptian King had to have fourteen ancestors — if there were not that number, it had to be made so — and in St. Matthew's Gospel the genealogy is divided into groups of fourteen. They are simply just ignorant!"

Apropos of the inadequacy of the official doctrine, I mentioned the existence of certain ancient sects who held that the Holy Spirit is feminine (this was a time-honoured Jungian cliché).

"But nowadays," I continued, "the Holy Spirit is right up in the air — purely masculine." As I said this, I visualised something like a long ruled line, extending through the atmosphere at a very high altitude, rather like the track of a jet. "It has no connection with anything underneath."

I don't think Jung liked my cliché very much.

"It is perfectly all right to have it masculine," he retorted. "You can have it as *masculine* as you like. But what on earth is the good of something masculine except by reference to something feminine? — That is the whole point of it!"

This was really quite an outburst. At the italicised word *masculine,* Jung switched on the full power of his very considerable vocal resources, and the point was rammed home with the force of a hammer.

"There was an old Norman French poet,"† he continued, "who

*Later, I tracked this reference down. The three are God, Ka-mutef and Pharaoh; Ka-mutef means "bull of his mother".

†This must have been Guillaume de Digulleville (see *CW* XI, p.68).

tells an amusing story. The Lord was talking to the Holy Spirit up in heaven, and he told him 'Well, now the time has come for us to become incarnate. So I want you to go down to earth and seek out a suitable candidate.' So the Holy Spirit went down, and he looked around, and eventually he saw Mary. Up he came again and told the Lord [here Jung put his finger alongside his nose with an indescribably comic gesture] 'Look! [pointing downwards with his finger to the earth] That's the one! *That's* the piece of goods for us!'"

"It was so *French!*" — and at this point Jung burst out into roars and roars of laughter, which went on and on, carrying everything before them like a gale. It was so irresistibly comic and infectious that I was caught up in it in spite of myself, and laughed with him again and again — though it was typical of my own puddenheadedness that the penny didn't drop for a moment or two.

What a marvelous laugh it was, though! I can still feel the impact of it as I write. I'm only thankful that I didn't let Jung down and disgrace myself for ever by completely failing to react to this test.

Jung told me that there is no mention of the Trinity in the New Testament, apart from one passage in St. John (Epistle I, 5, vii.) which is recognised to be an interpolation.

"Even the Roman Church recognised that," he said.

"Do they?" I replied (this was news to me).

"Oh yes," he said.

I mentioned that I was familiar with the passage (about the "three that bear record in heaven," etc.).

"Of course, it is quite impossible to write a biography of Jesus," Jung went on. "Do you know Albert Schweitzer's work? — you ought to read it."

I thought of *The Quest for the Historical Jesus* (which I hadn't read), but the title Jung was trying to quote was something different, possibly the title of the original German version.

Jung then went on: "Of course, if he [Jesus] had been just a Jewish rabbi, he would never have done anything. To come before the world, he had to become a myth."

Jung mentioned the case of the Jesuit who challenged him about how he could make out that Jesus was not fully human.* Jung explained to him that as, according to Catholic doctrine, Christ was not tainted by the *macula peccati,* he was not born into a corrupt body, as man is.† This clearly supports Jung's contention (in *Aion, C.W.* IX, pt. II) that Christ lacked a dark side. Thus, on the Church's own terms, Christ did not enter into the full human inheritance. The Jesuit had never thought of this point.

Jung told me several stories which are really illustrations of the same basic theme that had already cropped up in connection with Dr. Temple: what we might call the potential wisdom of the unconscious and the mortal peril we may run if we turn our backs upon its promptings.

"A colleague of mine," he said, "came to me four years ago and told me a dream in which a girl of twelve appeared. I told him his anima was twelve years old. He couldn't accept it.

"His wife, now—his wife saw it—she could see the point, but she dared not tell him. Now he is dead."

Jung explained to me the mechanism by which some of the these psychosomatic catastrophes are brought about. "The blood requires a certain degree of viscosity," he told me. "It has been proved that psychological conflicts of this type, in which there is a refusal to accept some insight, reduce the viscosity of the blood."

If we suppose that Jung's colleague was a psychologist and probably a qualified analyst at that, we can easily thought he knew all about the anima-he may even have been an authority on the subject. Obviously, then, the suggestion that his own female side was just twelve years old must have seemed peculiarly unacceptable to him. And yet it was apparently just this female side that was in need of development and attention.

---

*See Jung's letter of 14th, July 1960, p.128
†The doctrine of the Immaculate Conception means that Original Sin was, as it were, switched off at the conception of Mary, and Christ was therefore also "untainted" by it.

"A girl patient came to me," Jung continued. "She was Jewish, from Vienna. She was very pretty, well-educated and intelligent. She was having an analysis with a Freudian. She was quite a match for him intellectually. Then he got a countertransference and had to ask her to go, otherwise his marriage would be endangered. So she came to me.

"I had an extraordinary dream about her. I had never met her — there was just the name on the pad — Miss So-and-so, 4 o'clock tomorrow — but I dreamed that a woman patient came to me whose case I completely failed to fathom.

"Then she came — she had an intense anxiety condition. As that sort of thing is normally caused by a disturbance in the relationship with the father, I asked her about her father. She replied without any hesitation that her relationship with him was extremely good.

"I was baffled. I completely failed to understand her case. But if you dream something like this before it happens, that can be very significant.

"I *thought,* and finally it came into my mind that the relationship with the grandfather may sometimes have an effect in this way. The relationship with the grandfather may be very important. So I asked her about her grandfather.

"She lowered her eyelids — and that is a sign that one means to shut out something. I knew she was going to conceal something from me. She said 'Oh! I know nothing about my grandfather at all. I never had any contact with him.'

" 'But surely,' I said, 'your father must have told you something about him?'

" 'Oh yes,' she replied. 'Of course my father mentioned him. I knew he existed, but there was absolutely nothing important about him.'

"But I pressed her, and at last, with considerable resistance and shame, she told me that the family came from Galizien,* and that

---

*Galicia, a district in the former Austro-Hungarian Empire, now partly in the Soviet Union.

her grandfather had been one of the Hasidim, a living tradition within Judaism.

"I had an extraordinary dream," Jung continued. "I dreamed I was at a reception to which about fifty important personalities had been invited. And there, sure enough, was my woman patient — I was surprised. I would not normally invite one of my patients to such a reception. But there she was.

"Afterwards, when it was time to go, it was raining outside and she had no protection. I had no umbrella, but I looked around and found a umbrella. I didn't know the kind, but I pulled it out and made it work. [Jung demonstrated with movements of his arms how he apparently pulled out the shaft of this umbrella and made the spokes open out].

"Then, when I handed it to my patient," he went on, "I knelt right down... You see, she was a spiritual personage and couldn't accept it. She thought all that sort of thing was medieval nonsense and superstition. But in two weeks she was completely transformed. She was a transformed woman. The anxiety condition cleared up completely."

This story made a deep impression on me. It was fascinating to hear the aged psychiatrist (whose experience of analysis must have equalled even Freud's) reveal a glimpse of his technical expertise, as he did in the remark about the lowering of the eye-lids.

As it happened, I had heard of the Hasidim: my sister-in-law in New York had sent us a copy of Martin Buber's work on the subject. It was extremely interesting to me to hear Jung talk so seriously about a living tradition within Judaism.* In this case, the patient was able to accept and to act on the insight she had gained. But the next story Jung told me didn't have such a favourable outcome.

"I had another patient," Jung said, "an American Jew who was in the Diplomatic Service. He had a compulsion neurosis which

---

*This story later appeared in *Memories, Dreams, Reflections,* pp. 137-138. I have not altered my version in any way. I had the impression that this story meant a good deal to Jung — rather more than a casual reading of his memoirs might suggest.

prevented him from carrying out his profession. He was unable to accept the fact that he was a Jew.

"'Oh, no! Most of my friends are Catholics — we're all boys together,' he said.

"I took him for a fortnight — just long enough to show him why he didn't want to be cured. He was unable to accept the fact that he had wasted the best years of his life (twenty years) in a neurosis."

The point here, which comes out quite clearly, is closely akin to the point of the previous story. All men are brothers. This is true — and Jung's researches into the mythology of many nations both presuppose and support this conclusion. But we must not apply this truth mechanically, in an attempt to demonstrate that real differences do not exist. A man's own particular, distinctive inheritance may actually be the most important factor in his life. And to deny your own particular birthright — be it Jewish, African, working-class or Chinese — for the sake of the wrong kind of superficial adaptation to society may amount to denying your essential self — and that is quite capable of producing a neurosis.

I told Jung I found his criticism of the second half of my book most illuminating. I had assumed the psychological interpretation of God given in the first half as the basis for the second. But I hadn't realised how much my thought had been coloured by the conceptual world of the Anglican Eucharist.

Jung said he had dealt with the Mass in his writings, and mentioned something about the inadequacy of the orthodox interpretations. In self-defence, I explained that the Eucharist was a "living mystery" to me. Jung nodded, as though in assent. I said I had written to the Church authorities when my book was published, and had offered to leave the Church, as I didn't want to cause scandal when it became known that my views were so unorthodox. But they had wanted me to stay on. I was prepared to leave at any time — I just went on what guidance I had. I didn't go on any orthodox interpretations of the sacrament — I just took what came along. Jung assented, once more.

I went on to tell him that I'd been brought up to believe that everything is "nice," everybody is "nice," etc. "The result is," I said, "I've never been able to stick up for myself properly.

"I had a dream in which we were all to have tea with the Queen. We all had to be blindfolded for this. There was a great feeling of a presence, and apparently the Queen did pour tea. Afterwards, servants brought out cakes. Then a voice said, 'You've got to shout—and keep it up for a long time!'

"But I had a sexual emission, and this inhibited me from shouting. It wasn't really an emission—it was a fantasy," I explained. Jung understood this point perfectly; I had the comforting feeling that he knew all about it.

"I've never," I continued, "been able to have a job on a level up to my qualifications. I'm a simple *Angestellter* in the *Staatsdienst* [Civil Service]; a clerical officer, as it is called.

"If anyone here in Zürich is a hairdresser, and wants to work in England to improve his English, as many of them do, he has to send evidence of his qualifications and experience to the Ministry of Labour in London, and these *Zeugnisse,* etc., arrive on my table and I translate them.

"In a way, I'm like your first patient—the *petite fille de quinze ans,* who *sous le hypnose* was a *grande dame avec des manières hautaines et du baggage impressionant!*"*

I had lifted these French bits bodily out of the article in *Constellation,*† which I had bought in 1957 at the "French" in Old Compton Street and had recently reread. I was identifying myself with the heroine of this case—a rather backward dreamy adolescent girl who produced mediumistic phenomena in which she figured as a mature, brilliant woman of the world.

I could see Jung looking at me quizzically, in a slightly humorous or ironical way, as I said this. I don't know whether he got the precise reference, or whether he was in fact amused by

_____

*"a little girl of fifteen" who "under hypnosis" was a "great lady with aristocratic manners and an imposing array of knowledge."

†"Carl Jung: le tour du monde des rêves," by Jean-Gilbert Dumont, in *Constellation,* March 1957. See *C.W.* I, pp.3-88 for the whole story.

this rather comical way of talking about myself.

"This book I wrote was rather like that," I went on, "a compensation, like a dream, for my inferior position—so I did something grand! But since it's been published, I've got stuck!"

"Of course, when you write a book," Jung replied, "everything else is of secondary importance and is subordinate to that book. You are the book, it is a kind of case round you to which you are formed. When the book is finished, the form or cast is no longer needed. It is useless and can be discarded. But you are still identified with the book and therefore it is difficult to do this."

"I think what you said at the end of your second letter gives me a clue," I said. "'Not the approach to Christianity, but to God himself'—that, it would seem, is the ultimate question. But of course, I have to find out for myself first. I mustn't go starting by trying to write for other people first!"

Jung heartily concurred, "Then you will find places where something needs to be said," he remarked. This was his only specific reference to my future, and it pleased my very much.

As to the idea of the *Timor Dei* (Fear of God), Jung told me that to the primitives God was a great Rajah who had to be propitiated like a wrathful despot.

"A man met such a monarch once in the streets of a town," he said. "He fled away to avoid him down a side street. But the monarch saw him and went after him and caught him.

"'Why do you run away from me?' he asked.

"'Because I am afraid of you, Sire,' replied the man.

"Then the monarch was exceedingly angry. 'You mustn't do that! You must love me!' he replied."

I mentioned how Layard, in his study of the Stone Men of Malekula, in the New Hebrides (Jung obviously knew about this), had reported the existence of an amiable Father-God, of whom no-one took any notice. But Lev-hev-hev, the all-powerful malevolent Mother-Goddess, had to be placated with continual sacrifice.

Jung thoroughly agreed that this was so. He also told me about a passage in the Old Testament where the Lord said to Israel, "Yes!

I should like very much to go up to Jerusalem with you — but I'm afraid I might have an outbreak of my wrath and destroy you!" He said that the rabbis in their commentary on this passage explained that when Yahweh felt an attack of wrath coming on, he quickly got hold of the righteous and swept them under his throne, so that they'd be out of his sight and he wouldn't destroy them!

Jung's story about the colleague with the twelve-year-old anima awoke the memory of my own recent Jung-dream. So I told him about it.

"I dreamed of you sitting on a bench in front of your house, here, in Zürich," I said. "You had white hair and were extremely friendly. This was in compensation after the rather austere view I had in my conscious mind after your second letter — the Fear of God, etc. You told me, quite calmly, 'My mother has died. I just found her dead in bed.' I was astonished, and said that she must have been very old. Obviously, this dream cannot refer to you," I said. "It must refer to myself."

"And you projected it to me?" said Jung enquiringly, as if tentatively accepting my interpretation.

"I remember some years ago," I continued, "perhaps about 1954 — before I had any idea of visiting you in reality — I dreamed I was coming to visit you in Zürich. I met you just inside the front door, and the back of your head was that of a woman, with awful tangled, matted hair — in a terrible mess... Well, for many years I had this pretty bad mother complex, and I can only think that this second dream means that the mother complex in that form is now dead."

Jung entirely accepted this interpretation, and he went on to explain: "If the anima is projected to the mother and then becomes free, one may expect to find it reprojected, normally in the external world — for anything in the unconscious is discovered in the form of a projection."

I told Jung that I had had three great love-affairs: Catholicism (which represented my mother), German (my father), and his psychology, which in a way united both, since it explained to me what

Catholicism meant, and was, with its German background, connected with my father.

This was something I had more or less prepared to say; it was constructed, and I stumbled over it a little.

Jung understood perfectly well what I meant; but it was the only place in our conversation where I did not seem to have his entire and undivided attention. Interestingly, this happened at a moment when I was not being spontaneous—when it was not the living me that was speaking but an intellectual construct manufactured in the past.

I told Jung about the young man in the Swiss Travel Agency in London, where I had enquired about train-times and the cost of a ticket, etc. He knew Jung, and had asked me to ask him if he had altered his opinion about flying saucers.

"I had no opinion about them!," Jung replied. "I am just interested in them from the psychological side."

I gave Jung Ilse's greetings: "*Meine Frau gradisst Sie unbekannterweise*," I said. (Ilse had actually used the attractive and compendious German word *unbekannterweise,* and had commented on the fact that there is no equivalent word in English: you would have to say something like, "Though she hasn't the pleasure of knowing you personally"). Jung looked at me interestedly when I gave the greeting.

I went on to tell him that many of Ilse's colleagues had told her that they remembered Jung from the television interview with John Freeman. "He was the only one [in the "Face to Face" series] who *said* anything," one colleague remembered. These were quite ordinary people.

"Oh yes!," Jung replied, "he [John Freeman] is certainly a man—he has pulled quite a number of them over the grill.* I was afraid—I told Mr. Freeman so!"

There was a funny, Swiss up-and-down lilt in Jung's rather deep voice as he said these last two phrases. It was entirely unassum-

---

*Jung seems to have produced this amusing neologism out of a conflation of "grilling" and "hauling over the coals."

ing and democratic and I thought it had very great charm. And I admired the frank, matter-of-fact modesty with which he made this confession.

"But he treated me very kindly," Jung went on. "His questions made me stand up to them. I had to answer them and get out of them as well as I could."

I brought up the point about Freud's dreams, which Jung refused to discuss in the television programme. Jung misunderstood me here: "Oh, it is impossible in two minutes to describe the whole difference in scientific method. It is a scientific question that would take a long time."

I repeated the point about not revealing Freud's dreams on grounds of etiquette, and he answered, smilingly,

"Ah, yes, that too — it is not really the right time — etiquette!" He said this amusedly, and entirely without heavy, moralistic feeling.

Jung told me it was the ordinary people who were interested in him in Switzerland, also. The universities ignored him completely. "For them, my books are beneath consideration." He spoke about this lack of recognition without bitterness, but with a calm, slightly ironic kind of acceptance — as if he had long ago given up expecting anything different.

"A church dignitary once found a little book of mine on the table of a woman who had once been my patient," he told me.

"'Do you actually read this?' he asked her.

"'Oh yes! In fact, I find it quite helpful,' she replied.

"'But this is a *diabolical* work!' he exclaimed."

I mentioned the lights across the lake at night. Forming as they did a long band, they reminded me of what he had said in *Flying Saucers* about the picture by Yves Tanguy, where he confessed that he preferred the suggestion that the band of lights represented a city by night on the shores of the sea.

Jung smilingly accepted this piece of amateur detective work; he agreed that the lights on the lake had been his prototype. This is the only time I have traced a passage in Jung's writings back to his physical surroundings in Zürich.

I also mentioned Orfeo Angelucci (surprisingly appropriately
so called!) and his wonderful visions described by Jung in *Flying
Saucers*.

"Oh yes, all saccharin, all to music," Jung said. "He wrote to
me saying how much my mention of him in the book had helped
him in his career, etc.—quite ignoring the *tone* in which it was
written."

"Did you ever have any reaction from Fred Hoyle?" I asked him.

Jung's interpretation of the fantasy material in Hoyle's science
fiction story "The Black Cloud" was (to my way of thinking) shattering and tragic. I knew Jung had a great respect for Hoyle and
had read his scientific works; and I had wondered more than once
whether Hoyle in turn had read *Flying Saucers* and, if so, whether
Jung's interpretation had made any impression on him.

"Oh no!," Jung replied. "These people never take any notice
of me."

The whole tragedy of the modern world seems to me to be
summed up in these words. Science, the greatest achievement of
the human intellect, has not been able to come to terms with
wisdom.

Hoyle himself, without knowing it, expressed this most poig-
nantly in his story. The scientists who attempt to get into touch
with the Black Cloud (*i.e.*, the unconscious) and to assimilate its
tremendous insights die of brain injury caused by the stress of
the inflowing communication.

Our conversation had lasted for quite a long time by now, and
I was beginning to wonder when it would end. How different this
was from all those interviews in which your interlocutor advises
third parties that he will be finished with you in two or three
minutes' time! On reflection, I think I was actually a little bit worried. I was not used to anyone—let alone Jung—presenting me
with such a princely portion of his time! Once or twice I fancied
that Jung was going to bring matters to a conclusion; but no—
he still went on talking. At last, however, from somewhere in the

house a voice called out for him, and he called back loudly (in English), "Coming!" — very much as I do myself at home. It must have been Miss Bailey summoning him for lunch.

We got up, and as we were standing there, I handed over the Pelican edition of Rudolf Otto's *Idea of the Holy.* Jung said of course that he knew this book. So I drew his attention to the Appendix by the translator, where the point is made that English is richer in mystical terms than German.

Jung cottoned on to this at once, with interest. "I have never found any difficulty in talking to English people about things that are 'fey,'" he told me. "But with Germans, it is not easy; the language doesn't allow it There is a very good tradition in England in these matters."

Knowing contemporary England as I did, I said that this was wearing rather thin.

"But it is still there," Jung replied.

I complimented Jung on his excellent English (the conversation was conducted from start to finish entirely in English, on his side). Except in the solitary instance of the ecclesiastical technical term, he was never at a loss for a word. The only serious mistake I can remember was his amusing neologism: "pulling over the grill." The Swiss accent, when you noticed it at all, was charming: "in the book," he would say, the phrase being run off the tongue very trippingly and the vowel given the value of "Boo," as in English North Country dialect.

"It would be strange if I didn't speak it well," Jung replied, "as I have had so much to do with English people."

I drew his attention to the article by Smythies and Osmond in the April, 1959 number of *The Hibbert Journal* (I had put white strip paper markers in the publications to indicate the relevant passages).

His face lit up with recognition.

"Ah, yes! I know him," he exclaimed. (He didn't say which of the writers he meant).

"There is a certain berry which is chewed by the Indians and gives a drug akin to the adrenalins. It is mentioned by Aldous Huxley."

"Oh, yes! Mescaline," I said.

"Yes," he replied.

I pointed out that these writers had given him the credit for establishing the existence of the *mundus archetypus*.

"And they didn't think of sending me a copy," he said, rather sadly but quite without bitterness.

"Well, they say that is your greatness," I said.

Then I handed over my final present, *Lady Chatterley's Lover*. He smiled again—he was obviously familiar with the case. It was charmingly gracious, the way he accepted and found value in these really quite trifling little presents. I murmured something about thanking him for giving me so much of his time, and we shook hands, still by the window.

"A cold hand!," he remarked.

"Yes!—rather anxious," I said.

"I find that a warm hand means undisturbed good contact and no complexes," he said. "A cold hand means complexes."

"Oh, I've got plenty of complexes," I replied.

"A salad of complexes?" he said. As he stood there, his full stature and bigness was revealed. More than anything, he looked like one of the great nineteenth century explorers of Africa. We moved across the room, and he pointed out to me a largish, longish picture standing up against the opposite wall. A circular, mandala-like roundel occupied the centre of the design, subdivided organically like an anatomical section. It was a painting in the modern abstract style.

He told me that the artist, Richards, had two of his pictures purchased every year by the Tate Gallery. I remarked, in my usual obvious way, that it was a mandala, and he said "Yes! But why did he put a dog's penis in the middle?"

I looked, and thought I could roughly see a smallish round white elongated object, which I suppose was what Jung meant. "I wrote and told him about it," Jung went on. "I have had no reply. I hope he was not offended!"

This was said with very great humorous charm, and a kind of deprecatory humility which only the very hard of heart could fail to find attractive. We walked across towards the door, which was at the further end of the same wall.

"I hope you're comfortable at the Hotel Sonne," Jung said. "It's quite a simple place!"

"Oh, yes!" I said, enthusiastically, and with gratitude. "My bedroom looks out over the lake. It is number sixteen, and today is the 16th."*

"Encouraging," Jung said.

This was the word which my college friend and I used to use in the old Bayswater days to cheer each other up whenever anything came along which seemed positive in the life of either of us (we both had stiffish psychological difficulties to contend with). But he had died in the summer of that year, and there was no-one in my life now who used this word to me in quite that sense. It is a word of power to any nervous sufferer who's trying hard to wrestle with the serpent — and it certainly did me good to hear it applied to myself by Jung. It was very nearly the last thing he said to me.

Several pictures were hanging above the actual door of Jung's study. Outstanding among these was the original of the "Fire Sower" painting, which I knew from the illustration in *Flying Saucers* (Plate 2, opp. p.114). This struck me at once — it is incomparably larger and more imposing than the small, half-octavo photograph in the book. The colours in the original of this ghostly, longitudinal saviour-form are a wonderful rich, warm, vital, golden yellow, powerfully streaked (longitudinally again) with bright flowing red flame. It is a living figure, transcendently beautiful — an image one is not likely to forget.

---

*According to Jung, the number for is a symbol of totality; so much the more so, then, is four times four, or sixteen. The double occurrence of this multiple and its coincidence with my visit to Jung struck me (rightly or wrongly) as significant.

We remarked on this picture, and then went out though the door on to the landing. Opposite was the broad flight of stairs leading downwards, but I paused a moment and told Jung that my coat was in the little room on the left. I popped in and collected it, together with my gloves. Then we walked downstairs, with myself slightly in the lead. I wondered if Jung were gauging me from behind!

We parted on the lower level, with some slight awkwardness on my side. I made a motion to raise my hand and thank Jung once more. Jung turned away, the great old man — in height as in every other dimension towering above me.

Outside the house, I stood for a few moments looking at the dedicatory inscription on its oblong stone plaque, high up above that high front door. Now I had time to make it all out. It ran as follows:

CARL GUST JUNG ET EMMA RAUSCHENBACH HANC VILLAM MCM. VIII RIDENTI LOCO ET OTIOSO ERIG JUSS*

I walked up the steep drive to the street, crossed over and looked at the big electric clock on the garage. The time was ten minutes to one.

---

*Carl Gust. Jung and Emma Rauschenbach had this villa built in 1908 in this smiling and tranquil place.

XXXII
Conclusion _____

And so we come to the end — or nearly the end — of our story. It puts me in my time and place of course: the breakthrough of psychological analysis into middle-class life in England before, during and after the Second World War. What I've said has naturally been conditioned not only by my personal limitations and those of my class and period, but by the limitations of depth psychology in general. What I now want to do is to try to sum up — and then, truly, to conclude the story. I shall sum up, not unnaturally, in the terms I understand.

I was born a boy and technically normal — all parts present and in working order. And so it was my appointed task in life to play the man and encounter the woman outside. But I was delicate — thin bones and sensitive skin — and I had quite a rich and deadly vein of feeling inside me. Temperamentally, I was nearer to the woman than the man. Whatever happened, I was not going to

find it an easy matter to realise my manhood according to the
pattern. But caught as I was in actual fact in the jam between
my conflicting parents, I was bound to retreat from my oppressive father and cling to my loving but terrific mother. I was bound
to become a mother's boy.

My mother was the first woman I ever loved — the feminine prototype. And she was — and always remained — truly lovely. She was
the one who comforted me when I was in pain or trouble. She
was my refuge from the world, she coddled me, and such vitality
and masculintiy as I had were held in possession by her.

My strict father, who made me feel so guilty, was the last person I wanted in my Mummy-paradise. But he was also the first
man in my life — the masculine prototype. He stood for the stern
demands of reality and manhood. He seemed to be against me,
whereas my mother, warm and sheltering, seemed to be on my side.

But my father also loved me, and I loved him. He was a tall,
strong, splendid, red-faced man — with a straight nose. And there
was absolutely no alternative father. For a surprisingly long time,
in fact, he was literally the only man I knew. As a boy, I had to
model myself upon him. In despair I had to realise I would never
make the grade, and yet my father remained the model.

But my parents were united in one thing: the Christian
programme of goodness and healthy bourgeois hatred of sex. Here
was something I could — and did — become — a good, clean, obe-
dient little boy. In this way, I could keep my mother's favour, and
at the same time avoid offending my father too much. And it did
no violence to my own constitution. It was the inevitable but also
the perfect solution.

In Stage I, I'd failed to make the grade as a manly father's boy.
But in Stage II I *did* go over ideologically into my father's camp.
I accepted his values and supported his world. The way was open
for me to develop into a scholar and — for a time — a pilaster of
the British Empire.

But just as my father had been the serpent in my original
mother-paradise, so now my mother proved to be the snake in

the grass in my father's well-kept country garden. The passionate vitality of the natural London girl stormed uncontrollably against the prickly barriers of the schoolmaster's official philosophy.

My mother had the potential for a revolutionary alternative. But the time and the place were hopelessly wrong. The milieu was naturally determined by my father. It was an uncontaminated middle-class milieu of a kind almost unimaginable nowadays. The middle-class establishment ruled the roost, and my father was an authority figure in that establishment. Thus no real conflict in values was thinkable — and no real place for my mother's vitality. It was just a wicked, subversive disturber of the peace. And my own vitality, which was bound up with hers, had simply to be repressed and driven underground into the unconscious.

So we have what in effect is a two-tier universe. At ground level, a middle-class harmony of moderate conservatism presided over by the genius of my father. Underground, the ding-dong battle between my mother's revolutionary vitality and my father's traditionalism — the whole bottled up and sealed away in the unconscious. And my Self was parcelled out among the subdivisions of my world.

I lived very comfortably, on the whole, on the ground tier of my twostorey universe during the latency period — until, that is, the moment arrived when the onset of puberty shattered the hatches of the underworld.

When, after frightful wrestlings, I subdued the monster, I was tormented by the hornets of the repressed *libido sexualis,* translated into a kind of swarming anxiety. I was punished by the furies for an unconscious crime, committed in the conscious pursuit of virtue. Sincerely and revoltingly good though I was, I was up against a power far stronger than myself. I was not going to be permitted to eliminate my sexuality.

If I had to give a single short answer to the question, "What, in fact, *caused* your neurosis?," I should say, quite simply, *"the idea that masturbation is a terrible sin."* It was this single pseudo-religious conviction (which was equally and totally unwarranted and unchallenged) that gave the resultant conflict its unique ferocity, since it forced me to hurl my whole moral self into battle against my heftiest passion. It was this that tore my mental life into two and played lasting havoc with my nervous system. A more realistic attitude to sex, enlivened by a blessed gleam of humour and irony, would have reduced the problem to human proportions and prevented me, *e.g.,* from attempting suicide. There was no conflict between my parents on this issue; in fact, the entire milieu was united in repression.

The Blessed Virgin — a Mother, but without sex — opened the door for me into the Catholic Church. This was are more than a simple re-projection of the image of my personal mother. It was the entrée into a new paradise, a new realm, a new dimension.

Catholicism satisfied my need for a deep lodgement for my psyche. It's true, one or two essential items were lacking — for example, the free assent of my intelligence to the dogma. Even so, it was the only possible option for me, and it's not in the least surprising, really, that the Church became my world for the next nine years or so. In parts, I was surprisingly happy in my partial universe. But the snake in my Eden — this third time — was sex!

What had happened to my father under the new dispensation? On one level, I'd deserted him and retreated to Mother. The English public schoolboy's Protestantism and patriotism for the British Empire had vanished like vapours at the rising of the sun. Yet the Heavenly Virgin and our Holy Mother the Church were in a sense themselves accommodated inside my father's capacious mansion. I'd simply regressed half a millenium or more into the Catholic matrix of the same Western civiliation.

The Church itself was teeming with father-figures, but they were very different from my own father. They were transposed into the maternal key. They were servants, not of the Father-God of British Imperialism, but of the Mother-Goddess of Catholic Christianity. Here the Father was accommodated in the Mother's house — very much as the Holy Trinity, including God the Father, is sometimes portrayed in Catholic iconography as enclosed within the womb of the Blessed Virgin.

As usual, it was the serpent with his sting of discontent that finally expelled me from this Catholic paradise. I went to analysis to get rid, not of the Church, but of my neurosis. But actually, all the work I did at the Tavistock was a gnawing at the roots of my mother-fixation. And as the tree began to loosen its hold, so did the world it had built out around me. My "Surrender" poem shows me committed to the struggle for liberation, and though the mother-complex was still strong enough to make work on the land equivalent to incest, the vision of the priest and the choir of all humanity which I hatched out of a cleanway at the factory was, among other things, a valedictory at the passing of my *grande passion* for Catholicism. I never left the Church, but its influence receded; Freudian psychology stepped into the shoes of religion and became, for practical purposes, my *Weltanschauung*. And the German language became my physical passion.

However, the fates were not to be cheated so easily. I made a relative success of my life in the Army. But my marriage started of by kicking me violently downstairs into the black hole of misery in the unconscious, where I'd suffered such torment in my masturbatory period. The sexual problem, which, as sometimes happens, had been opened out but not resolved by psychological analysis, now came thundering upwards, overwhelmingly into consciousness. I was depressed and demoralised to the brink of despair.

Once again, I was ripe for conversion. But in my experience, what happens at times like these is not just conversion in the sense of a radical change of outlook, or of a *bouleversement* of the previously-held conscious attitude. When the psyche is shaken to the core and its very survival seems to be threatened, an archetype may thrust its fist through into consciousness — as if life itself were fighting for its life, so to speak.

As at Brighton in 1933, so at Hampstead in 1946, a revelation came my way from outside myself which exactly corresponded

to my inner need. Then, it was Catholicism: now, it was Jung.
Then it was a capacious though incomplete Mother-container for
my psyche: now I had a blinding flashpoint portrait of the unity
in totality of the psyche itself—and equivalent to what I'd experienced as "God" and been forced to reject as intellectually un-
tenable. The mother-wrappings of Catholicism had seemingly
contained something positive after all. Perhaps it was their function to protect this child till the moment was propitious for its
delivery.

My discovery brought together with a unifying bang my two
major, but opposing interests (psychology and religion). This was,
in itself, quite a big jump towards integration. Also (to shift the
metaphor once again) it uncorked the bottle of my resources as
a writer. My life's experiences started to flow out, not haphaz-
ardly, but coalescing into a definite pattern.

The whole new world now seemed populated by a marvellous
unity—so much so that, as I've said, it overflowed into writing,
and "The Idea of Humanity" was a result. One God, rather on
the Christian model, had apparently been restored to unify the
cosmos. But in truth, there was no kind of peace or unity, either
inside, in my psyche, or outside, in the world.

The dazzling glimpse of oneness I'd been vouchsafed was a kind
of therapeutic compensation for an actual, terrible, splitting
conflict. At Wilton Park, my sexual problem coincided with the
explosion of the Cold War—and at last the buried conflict fairly
burst through into consciousness.

My Big Dream of the white God and the brown Demoness
(1948) showed my father in marital conflict with my mother, myself in sexual conflict within my marriage, and the West in Cold
War conflict with Communist Russia. It was shattering, but it was
real—and the figures were so unmistakenly archetypal that I was
forced involuntarily to think of Jung. It was a tremendous advance to have got this thing constellated. The adversaries were
at last revealed. The Celestial Virgin-Mother of Catholicism wad
withdrawn her cohorts and vacated the field in favor of my ulti-

mate opponent—the chthonic brown Mother-Demoness who possessed my virility. She and the White Father were fighting it out.
The virulence of their slanging-match was so ferocious that the
cabin of the unconscious oscillated violently. But the psyche was
strong enough to contain this conflict, and the Father, who
represented my own sex, actually succeeded in silencing his fulminating antagonist. Once again there was a creative intervention from the side of the unconscious. The Shadow, in the shape
of a man-faced serpent, began to detach itself from the Mother-
Anima and to transfer some of its energies towards the schematic White Father.

What I actually sent to Jung in October, 1948 was the whole
bloated typescript of my "Idea of Humanity" *plus* a cover letter
telling him about my Big Dream. The first was the precipitate of
a vision of God as the unity in totality of the human psyche; the
second laid bare my own psyche as actually split from top to bottom. This initiated a personal dialogue between Jung and myself.

As a result, I went into analysis with Mrs. Hella Adler, and
this led on to two other developments. I started my apprenticeship as a writer on psychology by recording and interpreting my
own dreams. And I embarked upon a corporate relationship with
Jung's ideas through Jung's own books and those of some other
members of his school. No longer was I a lonely Pauline figure.
I was a member, though a semi-detached one, so to speak, of the
Jerusalem Church.

My analysis had to be suspended in 1953, but I went on writing out my dreams, and my transference to Jungian psychology
remained in full swing. More specifically, it had become a personal transference to Jung. My first dream of a visit to Jung occurred on 22nd March, 1954. The opposites were still clearly
distinguishable—male and female, light and darkness, order and
chaos—and they were still far from being harmoniously recon-
ciled, but Jung appears as a kind of uniting symbol, combining
the contraries.

The following year, I launched upon the *Intelligent Agnostic,*

my second grand assault on book-writing. With six years' apprenticeship behind me, I was able to attempt, however imperfectly,
a Jungian critique and interpretation of Christianity. I bundled
up three of my creative obsessions — religion, psychology, and
writing — and offered the public a sort of do-it-yourself course in
ideological psychotherapy. In the process I had to come to terms
with Christianity myself and find out what it all meant to me personally. Apart from God, prayer and morals reinterpreted inwardly
in terms of the total personality, much of it seemed to boil down
to the Eucharist, which itself turned out to be a psychic death
and rebirth of the personality, dramatically enacted through a mystery of transformation.

The publication of my *Agnostic* was the greatest success I had
achieved in my life up to that moment. It was almost as if I'd
made my bow before the world at last. But the success was abrupt-
ly followed by failure. I'd crammed all I'd got into that bomb-
shell of a masterpiece and was correspondingly depressed and
deflated when even this superhuman exertion failed to blast me
out of my cramped little funk-hole. I couldn't deidentify myself
with the book, and I couldn't either write another or find an alternative outlet. I'd come to a standstill; I'd lost my way.

At last, after a year's wait, I succeeded in bringing Jung himself into action. His tremendous response transformed the whole
situation. He confessed to me that my book had touched him
deeply at a time when, in his extreme old age, he himself was lonely
and disappointed. I was overwhelmed and came right out of my
carapace to meet him.

The immediate effect of this was exhilarating. It was as if I'd
been right up on the windy heights, drinking draughts of mountain air. I'd touched greatness, and momentarily, at any rate, the
barriers had dropped away.

When I reached home I wrote down the whole of the conversation between Jung and myself. I managed to get it all onto paper within a month, though there was a hard tussle between that
and the requisite Christmas mail, which I'd deferred to go out

to Zürich.

At some point or other I then conceived the notion that if and when Jung should die, I would bundle up my life and his whole impact on it into a single big case-history, and offer myself hopefully to the public as a guinea-pig illustration of Jung's psychology.

I don't honestly think I *wished* Jung to die. When the news of his death came through, less than six months after I met him, it came as a personal stab to me. It seemed as if he'd always been there, the wise old man of Zürich, and it was always possible that he might still say or do something. This did keep on happening, surprisingly often, right up to the end. But now he was gone forever, and there was nobody—but nobody—to take his place. It was a feeling of ultimate loneliness for me, but none the less poignant for that. For the future I should have to provide my own guidance and orientation. In a sense, I should have to become the wise old man myself. However, a certain amount of heart-searching had to be done along the stages of this process; among other things, I eventually lost my naive faith in Jung.

More than one rivulet contributed to this stream. There was a battle between the generations in English Jungian psychology; the younger generation was far more socially-minded than the old guard. I was on the extreme outer fringe of this conflict, but both in discussions and in the pages of the *Journal of Analytical Psychology* the voice of the young men had its impact upon me. It was a painful but salutory experience. My image of Jung was severely shaken. It was as if he stood for the kind of idea of introversion which was now—and rightly—being cast out.

How far is this true of Jung himself? As a matter of fact, far from being a negative quantity, Jung had outstanding social gifts in the shape of spontaneity, humor, and the capacity to be wholly *with* whoever he was with at a particular moment. He had a really uncanny intuition for the other person's real needs and situation. His witty conversation captivated Freud when they met, and it was not for nothing that Freud selected Jung to be his own spiritual son and heir.

And yet, on the whole Jung didn't choose to be popular. The reason for this is, I believe, very simple. He was an introvert, a genius, and a man with a mission. For him, work—meaning psychology—came first, and social intercourse a bad second. There is nothing uniquely horrible about this; any person who is engaged on a great creative enterprise is liable to be confronted with the same problem. To take one notable instance, Mrs. Charles Darwin performed the wifely function of screening her husband from social engagements which might have distracted him from his biology. It is just as likely that social life will interfere with concentration as the work itself will suffer for lack of social contacts.

Jung had a rich and abundant life, and a richly and abundantly productive one. It certainly cannot be said of him that he failed to produce the work of which he was capable. And yet when he wrote to me, "I have failed in my foremost task, to open people's eyes to the fact that man has a soul and that there is a buried treasure in the field...," he was, I believe, telling the truth; in a sense, he was so supremely concentrated on pursuing and formulating his researches that he lost sight of the audience for whose benefit he was doing this. He had been successful on the *objective* side: he had tracked down the quarry to its ultimate hiding-place, and expressed the results in terms of his psychology. But he had not been successful in opening people's eyes, *i.e.,* in transmitting his discoveries to the public.

Scientifically, Jung was an exile, yet he himself did little to counteract this situation. In any branch of knowledge it is necessary to know what is being written. Apart from *The Future of an Illusion* and *Moses and Monotheism,* Jung did not, apparently, read any of Freud's works written later than the split between the two men. Nor did he take very much trouble to keep abreast of the work done by other schools. His contacts were with spiritual philosophy and religion—and, interestingly enough, with physics.

It is quite true that Jung literally didn't have time for anything unrelated to his ruling passion. Much the same, incidentally, applies to Freud himself and most of the other first-generation pioneers. And it can be argued that Jung did in fact possess all the contacts he required for his unique speciality. But he still could have employed a scout or two to spy out the surrounding countryside for him. This would have kept him in closer touch with those practitioners of psychology and members of the educated public who didn't happen to share his special interests.

At the end of his long life, when the war was over and the last of his great researches was completed, I believe Jung became increasingly aware of the gap which separated his revolutionary achievement from the world of scientific and humanistic learning—for whom, after all, it was intended.

He was always recognised as a world figure, and all through his life he responded to requests to write expositions of his psychology for the benefit of the layman. At the same time, he had never seen himself as a cosmic celebrity whose opinions were likely to alter the destiny of nations. Yet the fact remained that he had now produced a series of major works in which he had documented the major discoveries of his maturity—and no-one had taken any particular notice.

Jung's temperament certainly contributed to this situation. And yet, paradoxically, there were few people better equipped than he was to redress the imbalance. In his eighties, Jung conquered his dislike of publicity and appeared before the world in person as the most convincing advocate of his psychology. It looks as if the quite considerable efforts Jung made in the last four years of his life to rupture the charmed circle of isolation and misunderstanding were by no means without effect, and that they have, to some extent at any rate, fulfilled his dream of speaking to a wider audience.

. . . .

We now have to return from C.G. Jung to the far less fascinating subject of myself. Jung's image provided a kind of mould or casting—a scaffolding, if you prefer—within which my split psyche could to some extent be reunited. As I see it, the cast was provided by the archetype of the Self projected onto Jung. In loose but unportentious language, Self + Jung = Split + Splint. The imagery to my mind supplies the mechanics of the process; the vehicle was an actual, living relationship.

We all have to project, otherwise we would never grow up. The process in itself is entirely normal; the only abnormality was that *I* was sick. But we all have also to withdraw our projections, otherwise our growing pains will speedily congeal into the crotchety rheumatics of premature senescence.

Before the end of analysis, something is supposed to happen which is known as the dissolution of the transference. The patient is not "cured" until he has dismissed the doctor. This I take to be an example of a general law. I too had to say goodbye to Jung — or at least to my tighthugged illusion of him. And the parting was not such a sweet sorrow, either.

Naturally, the new motif of disengagement from Jung had an effect on the *Encounter With Jung* I was writing. At times the work practically came to a standstill, but the impulse never died — it simply slipped below the surface. Later it bobbed up again, reinvigorated and in a noticeably less immature form.

But what about the second term in this extraordinary relationship? What was my aim in the portrayal of Eugene Rolfe? No doubt, here as always, there was a commingling of motives — some may have been slightly less unworthy than others. It is certainly true that I didn't intend to idealise, at least not in the traditional meaning of the term. In fact I was almost unecessarily severe on myself at times. Yet I had chosen my ground with deep unconscious craftiness: by exhibiting my life as a casehistory, I'd removed myself (or so it could be supposed) from the harsher categories of moral judgement; and I might even hope that the odder my conduct was, the more interesting it would be found from the psychological viewpoint.

"You've got to shout," a voice in a dream once told me.

"You've got to shout — and keep it up for a long time!"

My claim is, briefly, that *Encounter With Jung* is a modest attempt at complying with this injunction.

Index